Yesteryear
in
Cross Stitch

Yesteryear
in
Cross Stitch

Debbie Minton

COLLINS & BROWN

To Jane and Will, for all their wonderful help throughout this book

First published in Great Britain in 2000
by Collins & Brown Ltd
London House
Great Eastern Wharf
Parkgate Road
London SW11 4NQ

135798642

British Library Cataloguing-in-Publication Data:
A catalogue record for this book
is available from the British Library.

ISBN: 1 85585 7189

Editor: Heather Dewhurst
Designer: Sara Kidd
Photographer: Shona Wood

Reproduction by Hong Kong Graphic and Printing Ltd
Printed and bound in Hong Kong/China
Distributed in the United States and Canada by Sterling Publishing Co,
387 Park Avenue South, New York, NY10016, USA

Contents

Introduction

At the end of a century it's lovely to look back to the way of life a hundred years ago and think about how different everything was then: children playing happily in the street or in the nursery, having fun with simple wooden toys, adults sitting by the fireside or in the garden, stitching or reading. Compared to the busy lives we all lead now, in years gone by there seemed to be more time to enjoy simple everyday pleasures. The projects in this book, *Yesteryear in Cross Stitch*, are designed to provide a glimpse back in time to those nostalgic days of yesteryear. I thoroughly enjoyed designing the projects with children in them for this book; they seem to have a look of total innocence about them. I have fond memories of many of the old-fashioned toys featured in these designs. When I was little, my father built me a beautiful dolls' house. The front and back doors opened and the roof came off to give an attic playroom. I had hours of fun playing with all my dolls in each room and imagining the dolls as a real family – I used to make tea parties for them, and even tell them off when they were naughty (really I did!). My dolls' house is in the loft now and on the odd occasions when I actually go up there, I always take a peep inside the house to make sure that everyone inside is OK. I like to think that we are all children at heart, which is often preferable to being a grown-up all the time!

In researching for this book, I spent hours and hours wandering through bookshops and museums in search of dress fashions and hair styles suitable for the period. In doing so, I have come to appreciate the skill that went into the stitching of the elegant gowns worn then – the exquisite detailing must have taken years of practice. There is one project in particular, A Skaters' Waltz (see page 72), which I think is particularly nostalgic. It was actually inspired by a trip to New York at Christmas time, where I spent one evening watching the skaters on the ice rink at the Rockafeller Center. The skaters there looked so graceful with their fur-trimmed coats and muffs that I had to reproduce the image. I hope the designs in this book reflect the sense of style of the clothes of yesteryear.

Many of the designs in this book are stitched on Aida and are easy to stitch.

Although some use linen, you can stitch them on Aida if you prefer. Don't be afraid of linen – it is so beautiful and soft to stitch on and produces very subtle results. After a while you will get used to working over two squares instead of one. I hope you enjoy working on the projects I have designed for you, and that in spending time in the everyday pleasure of stitching you appreciate your glimpse into the days of yesteryear.

Summertime Swinging

This delightful project expresses the sheer joy of childhood. With the sun on her face and the wind in her hair, this girl is having a wonderful time. To achieve a more old-fashioned look, stitch the design on beige or ivory linen.

ACTUAL DESIGN SIZE
8½ x 7½in (22 x 19cm)

MATERIALS
- 1 piece of 16-count Aida in white measuring approximately 13¼ x 12¼in (33 x 30.5cm)
- No 24 tapestry needle

INSTRUCTIONS
Mark the centre of the chart. Find the centre of your fabric and make long tacking stitches across and down. Using two strands of stranded cotton (except for backstitching where you use one strand only) begin your work following the chart. For full instructions for cross stitches, backstitches and special

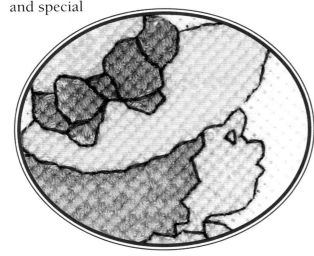

The sweet, fresh innocence of youth

shaping stitches see the *Techniques* section on pages 121-126 of this book.

THREADS

DMC Colour	Metres
420 toffee brown	7
433 brown	1
470 green	2
676 pale mustard	1
729 mustard	1
745 dark straw yellow	2
746 cream	2
799 cornflower blue	1
800 forget-me-not blue	1
801 dark brown	1
809 blue	1
898 very dark brown	1
986 dark forest green	2
988 light forest green	6
3046 khaki	1
3074 light khaki	1
3770 flesh	1
3799 charcoal grey	3
3823 pale banana yellow	5

COLOUR FOR BACKSTITCHING
Backstitch the swing ropes using two strands of 3799.
Backstitch all other outlines using one strand of 3779.

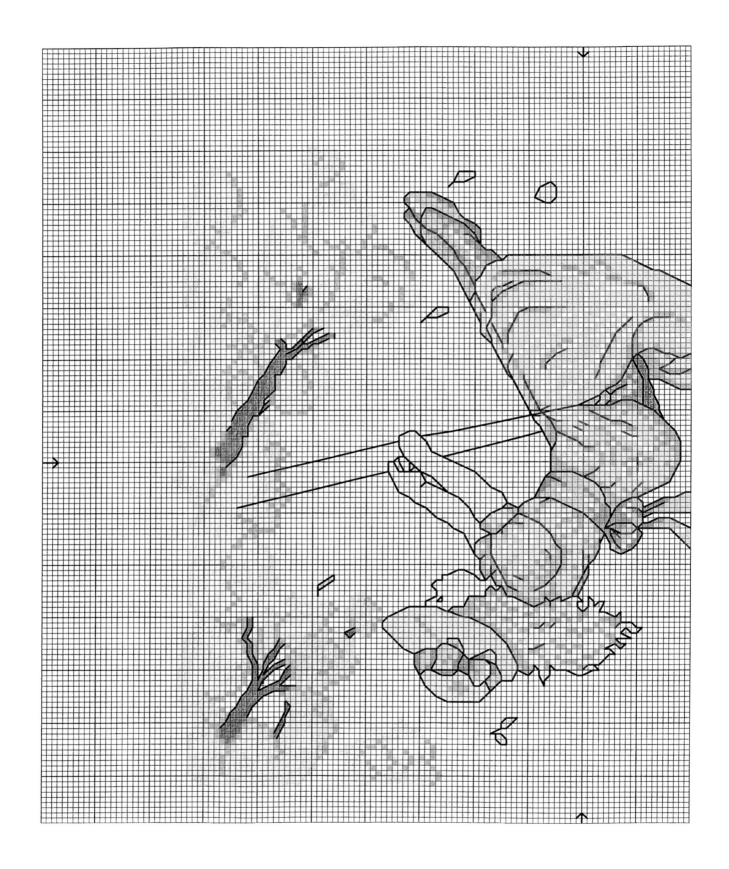

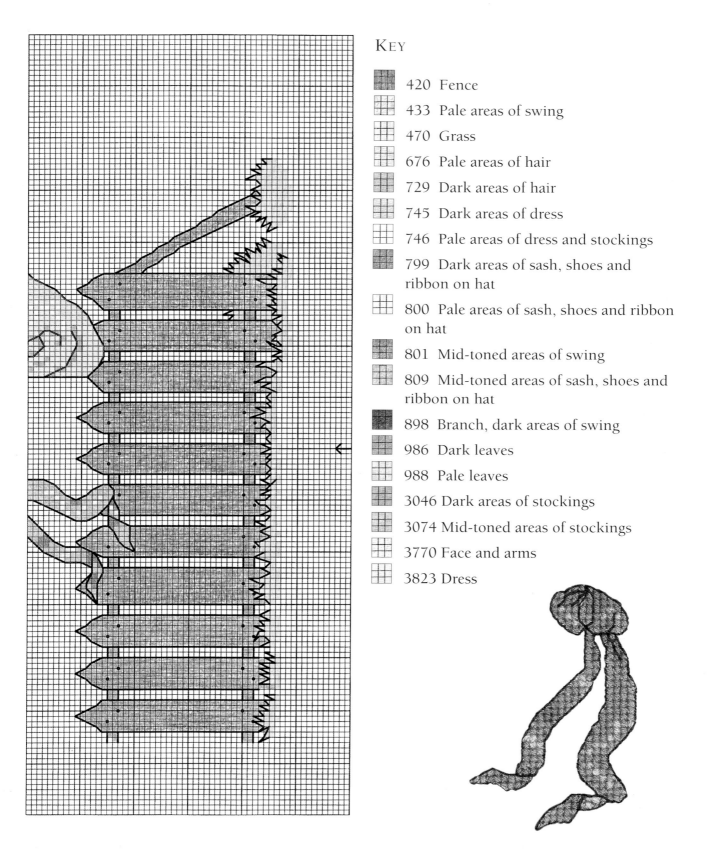

KEY

420 Fence

433 Pale areas of swing

470 Grass

676 Pale areas of hair

729 Dark areas of hair

745 Dark areas of dress

746 Pale areas of dress and stockings

799 Dark areas of sash, shoes and ribbon on hat

800 Pale areas of sash, shoes and ribbon on hat

801 Mid-toned areas of swing

809 Mid-toned areas of sash, shoes and ribbon on hat

898 Branch, dark areas of swing

986 Dark leaves

988 Pale leaves

3046 Dark areas of stockings

3074 Mid-toned areas of stockings

3770 Face and arms

3823 Dress

A Surprise Gift

The shy expression on this young boy's face is very appealing. The charming cut of his clothes and the beautifully subtle colours of the fabric place him in the early part of the century, perhaps after a day at the fair. For an authentic Victorian flavour, frame this picture in a dark wooden frame.

ACTUAL DESIGN SIZE
7 x 2¼in (17.5 x 5.5cm)

MATERIALS
- 1 piece of 18-count Aida in cream measuring approximately 12 x 7in (30 x 17.5cm)
- No 24 tapestry needle

You'll never guess what I'm holding behind my back . . .

INSTRUCTIONS
Mark the centre of the chart. Find the centre of your fabric and make long tacking stitches across and down. Using two strands of stranded cotton (except for backstitching where you use one strand only) begin your work following the chart. For full instructions for cross stitches, backstitches and special shaping stitches see the *Techniques* section on pages 121-126 of this book.

THREADS

DMC Colour	Metres
301 dark ginger	1
400 chestnut brown	1
500 dark pine green	1
501 pine green	1
502 light pine green	1
738 dark cream	1
739 ivory	1
761 pink	1
838 chocolate brown	1
839 dark beige	2
840 mink	2
841 beige	1
3328 dark raspberry	1
3770 flesh	1

COLOUR FOR BACKSTITCHING
Backstitch all outlines using 838.

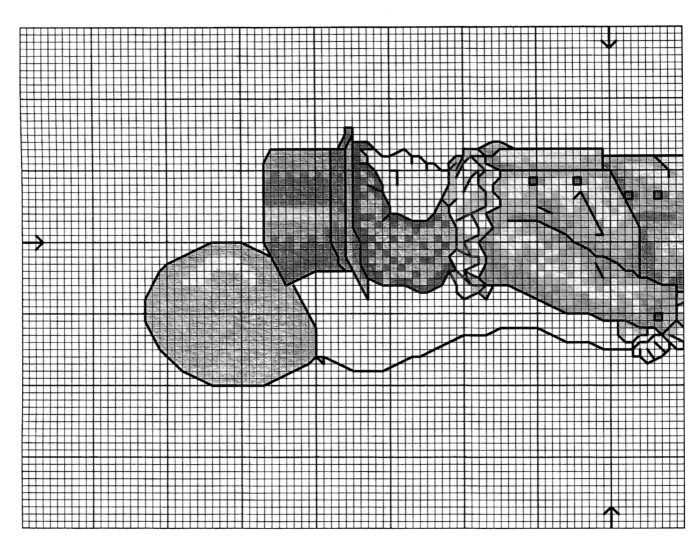

KEY

301 Light areas of hair

400 Dark areas of hair, and buttons

500 Dark areas of jacket

501 Mid-toned areas of jacket

502 Light areas of jacket

738 Dark areas of ruff, cuffs and stockings

739 Pale areas of ruff, cuffs and stockings

761 Highlight on balloon

839 Dark areas on hat, trousers and shoes

840 Mid-toned areas on hat, trousers and shoes

841 Pale areas on hat, trousers and shoes

3328 Balloon

3770 Face and hands

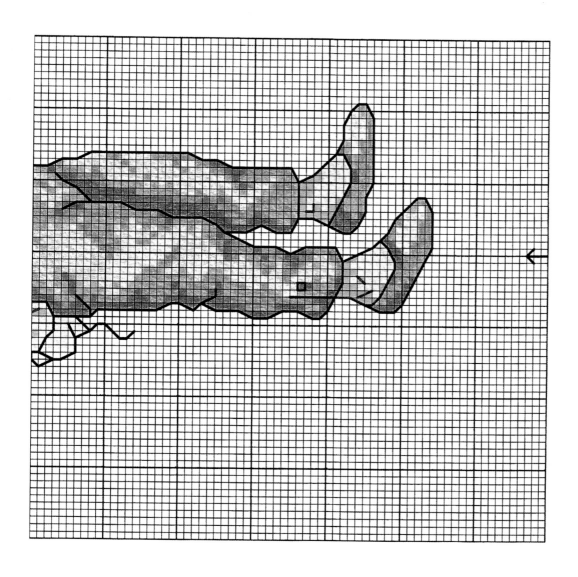

Bowling the Hoop

This delightful scene captures the playfulness and fun of a carefree childhood. The boy from a bygone era plays with a hoop while his dog runs along beside him.

ACTUAL DESIGN SIZE
9 x 8in (22.5 x 20cm)

MATERIALS
- 1 piece of 16-count Aida in white measuring approximately 14 x 12¾in (35 x 32cm)
- No 24 tapestry needle

INSTRUCTIONS
Mark the centre of the chart. Find the centre of your fabric and make long tacking stitches across and down. Using two strands of stranded cotton (except for backstitching where you use one strand only) begin your work following the chart. For full instructions for cross stitches, backstitches and special shaping stitches see the *Techniques* section on pages 121-126 of this book.

The days when all little boys wore hats

THREADS

DMC Colour	Metres
304 crimson	1
310 black	1
311 midnight blue	1
312 cornflower blue	2
322 blue	1
334 light blue	1
415 grey	1
420 toffee brown	6
470 green	1
676 pale mustard	1
712 light cream	2
729 mustard	1
738 dark cream	1
739 ivory	1
814 burgundy	1
815 claret	1
816 maroon	1
898 dark brown	2
986 dark forest green	1
988 light forest green	8
3325 powder blue	1
3755 sky blue	1
3774 oyster	1
3799 charcoal	3

COLOURS FOR BACKSTITCHING
Backstitch the shoes using one strand of 310.
Backstitch the hoop using two strands of 3799.
Backstitch all other outlines using one strand of 3799.

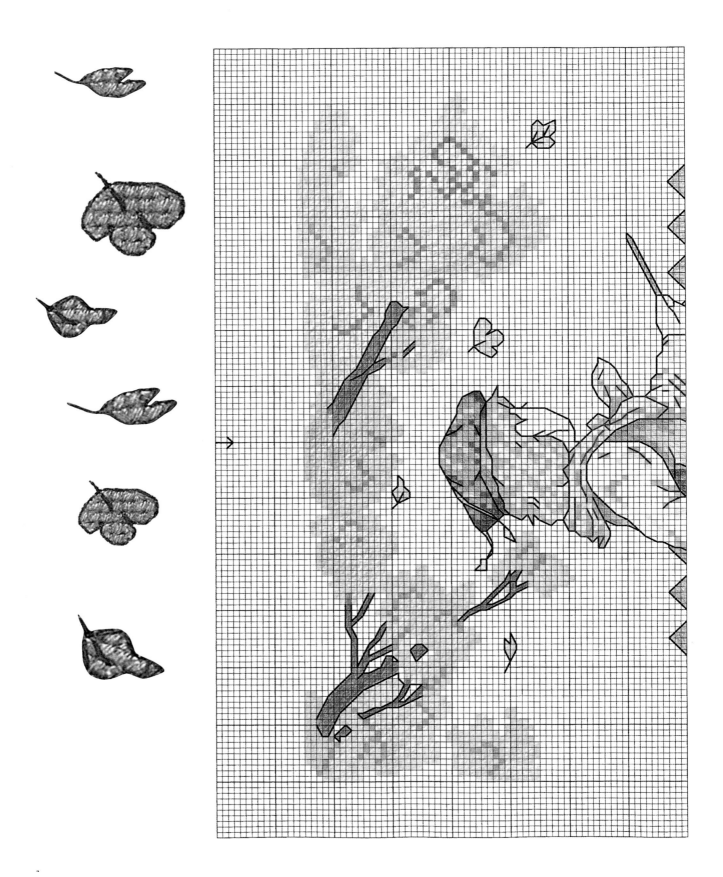

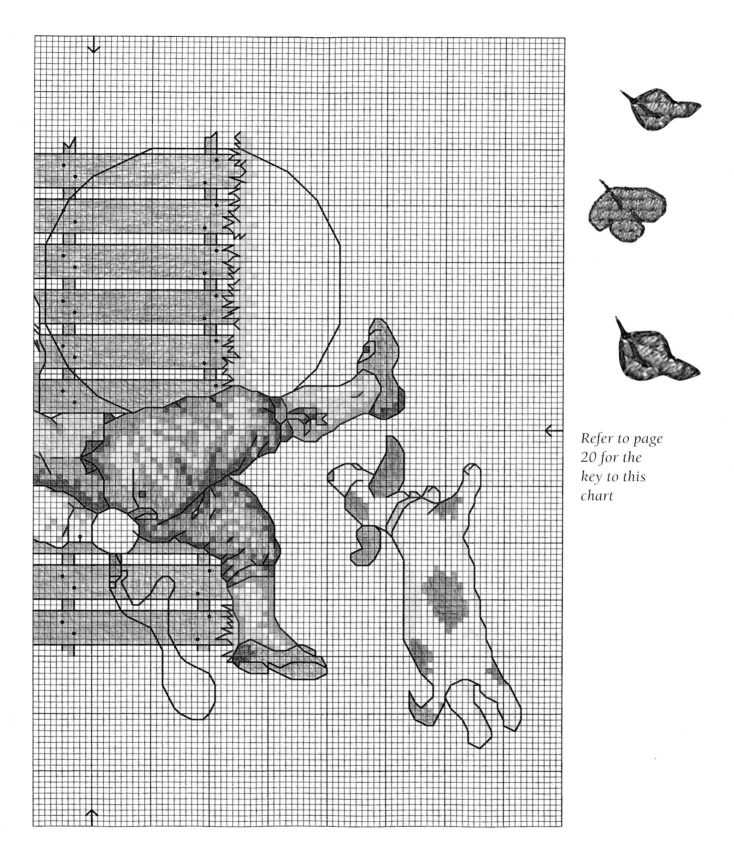

Refer to page 20 for the key to this chart

KEY

304 Pale areas of hat and waistcoat, dog's collar

310 Heels of shoes, centre of shoe buckle

311 Shading on breeches

312 Mid-toned areas of breeches

322 Pale areas of breeches

334 Dark areas of neckerchief and stockings

415 Shadow

420 Fence

470 Grass

676 Pale areas of boy's hair

712 Pale areas of shirt and dog

729 Dark areas of boy's hair, shoe buckles

738 Dark areas on shirt

739 Mid-toned areas of shirt, shading on dog

814 Shading on hat and waistcoat

815 Mid-toned areas of hat and waistcoat

816 Light areas of waistcoat

898 Dog's ears and patches in fur, branches

986 Dark areas of leaves

988 Pale areas of leaves

3325 Pale areas of stockings

3755 Pale areas of neckerchief, mid-toned areas of stockings

3774 Boy's face and hands

3799 Patches on dog's fur, shoes, stick, catapult

Life's simple pleasures always bring a smile to one's face

Wreathed in Flowers

Pincushions are domestic reminders of times gone by, when embroidery was used to decorate everything from clothing to bedlinen. The colours on this pincushion stitched against black Aida are stunning. This pincushion is diamond shaped, but you could make a circle or a heart if you prefer.

ACTUAL DESIGN SIZE
3³/₄ x 3³/₄in (9.5 x 9.5cm)

MATERIALS
● 1 piece of 16-count Aida in black measuring approximately 8¹/₂ x 8¹/₂in (22 x 22cm)
● No 24 tapestry needle
● 1 piece of black backing cloth measuring approximately 5 x 5in (12.5 x 12.5cm)
● Polyester filling
● Black tassel
● Black braiding

INSTRUCTIONS
Mark the centre of the chart. Find the centre of your fabric and make long tacking stitches across and down. Using two strands of stranded cotton (except for backstitching where you use one only) begin your work following the chart. For full instructions for cross stitches, backstitches and special shaping stitches see the *Techniques* section on pages 121-126.

THREADS

DMC Colour	Metres
470 green	1
471 olive green	1
676 pale mustard	1
746 cream	1
3705 dark pink	1
3706 pink	1
3713 pale pink	1

COLOUR FOR BACKSTITCHING
Backstitch the flower stems using 470.

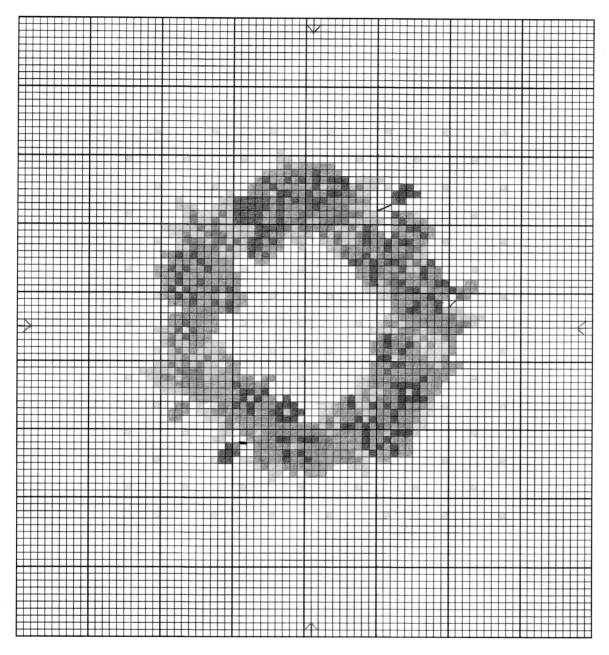

KEY

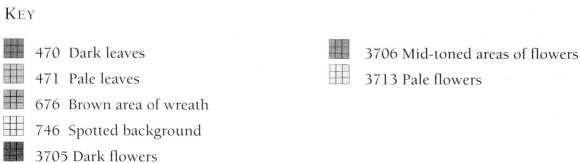

470 Dark leaves

471 Pale leaves

676 Brown area of wreath

746 Spotted background

3705 Dark flowers

3706 Mid-toned areas of flowers

3713 Pale flowers

Beneath the Wisteria

This serene design depicts a lady of leisure sitting in a swinging hammock, quietly reading, while the scented wisteria blooms overhead and a topiary tree stands guard at one side. Backstitch is used to outline the twining stems of the wisteria branch and the formal shape of the topiary tree.

ACTUAL DESIGN SIZE
9¼ x 7¼in (23 x 18.5cm)

MATERIALS
- 1 piece of 18-count Aida in white measuring approximately 14 x 16in (35 x 40cm)
- No 24 tapestry needle

INSTRUCTIONS
Mark the centre of the chart. Find the centre of your fabric and make long tacking stitches across and down. Using two strands of stranded cotton (except for backstitching where you use one strand only) begin your work following the chart. For full instructions for cross stitches, backstitches and special shaping stitches see the *Techniques* section on pages 121-126 of this book.

THREADS

DMC Colour	Metres
208 dark purple	2
209 purple	2
210 light purple	1
349 dull red	1
415 light grey	1
433 medium brown	2
434 pale brown	2
597 dark duck egg blue	3
598 duck egg blue	5
712 cream	1
729 mustard	2
744 yellow	1
801 dark brown	1
919 terracotta	1
920 dark cinnamon	1
922 cinnamon	1
936 dark sage green	1
937 sage green	1
986 dark forest green	3
987 forest green	3
988 light forest green	1
3770 flesh	1
3799 charcoal grey	5
3808 dark petrol blue	1
3809 petrol blue	1
3810 dark turquoise	2
3811 aqua	3
3823 pale yellow	1
3829 dark mustard	1

COLOUR FOR BACKSTITCHING
Backstitch all outlines using 3799.

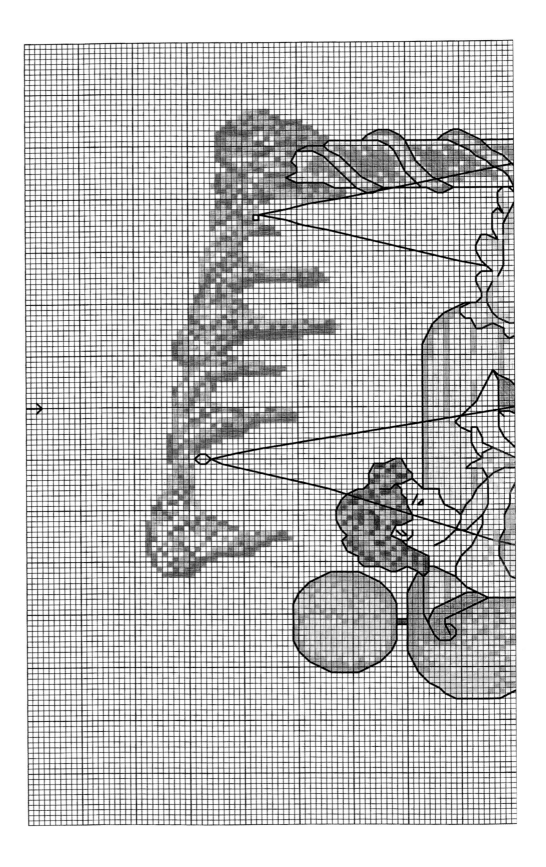

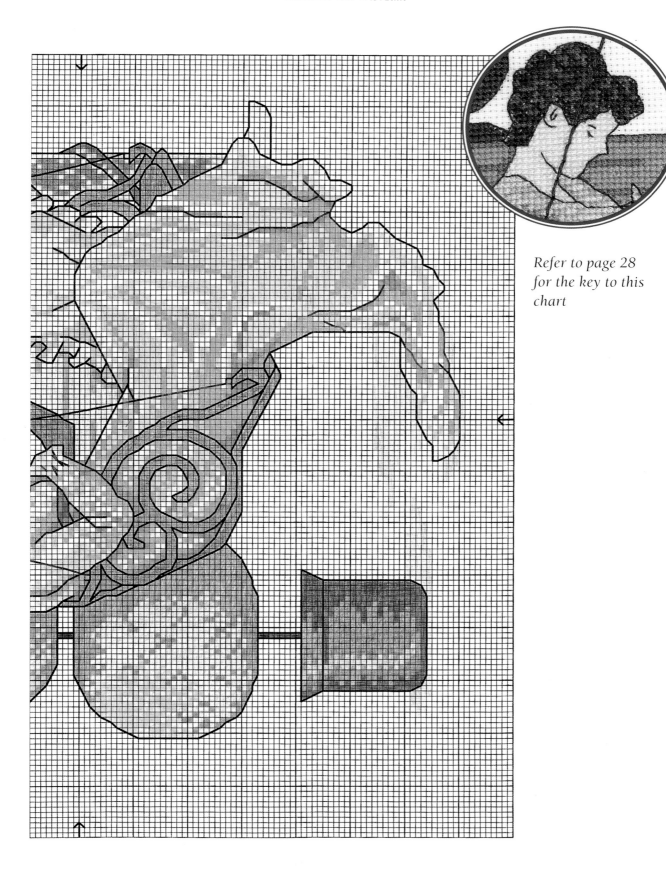

Refer to page 28 for the key to this chart

KEY

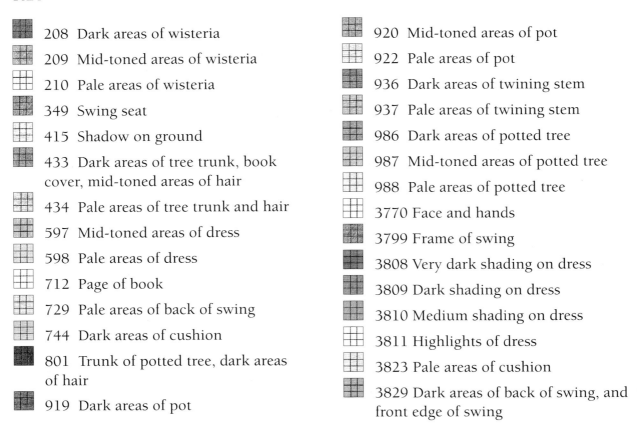

208 Dark areas of wisteria

209 Mid-toned areas of wisteria

210 Pale areas of wisteria

349 Swing seat

415 Shadow on ground

433 Dark areas of tree trunk, book cover, mid-toned areas of hair

434 Pale areas of tree trunk and hair

597 Mid-toned areas of dress

598 Pale areas of dress

712 Page of book

729 Pale areas of back of swing

744 Dark areas of cushion

801 Trunk of potted tree, dark areas of hair

919 Dark areas of pot

920 Mid-toned areas of pot

922 Pale areas of pot

936 Dark areas of twining stem

937 Pale areas of twining stem

986 Dark areas of potted tree

987 Mid-toned areas of potted tree

988 Pale areas of potted tree

3770 Face and hands

3799 Frame of swing

3808 Very dark shading on dress

3809 Dark shading on dress

3810 Medium shading on dress

3811 Highlights of dress

3823 Pale areas of cushion

3829 Dark areas of back of swing, and front edge of swing

The perfect way to spend a golden afternoon

In the Country

Sitting by the lakeside watching swans and reading a book seems an ideal way to pass a warm summer's afternoon. Notice the period detail of the cushion the girl is sitting on – essential for protecting the delicate fabric of her dress. For a smaller design suitable for a card, stitch just the swan.

ACTUAL DESIGN SIZE
10 x 11½in (25 x 29cm)

MATERIALS
- 1 piece of 16-count Aida in white measuring approximately 14¾ x 16¼in (37.5 x 40.5cm)
- No 24 tapestry needle

INSTRUCTIONS
Mark the centre of the chart. Find the centre of your fabric and make long tacking stitches across and down. Using two strands of stranded cotton (except for backstitching where you use one strand only) begin your work following the chart. For full instructions for cross stitches, backstitches and special shaping stitches see the *Techniques* section on pages 121-126 of this book.

THREADS

DMC Colour	Metres
208 purple	1
310 black	1
311 mid-blue	1
317 dark grey	1
336 dark blue	4
469 olive green	2
470 green	1
471 light olive green	8
597 dark turquoise	1
598 turquoise	2
712 cream	1
721 dull orange	1
762 grey	2
813 royal blue	3
823 navy blue	3
827 blue	4
828 pale blue	8
937 sage green	2
938 brown	2
948 pale salmon pink	3
951 dark flesh	1
3341 peach	3
3347 dark pistachio green	1
3371 dark brown	1
3770 flesh	1
3799 charcoal grey	4
3811 aqua	1
3824 pale peach	5
White	3

COLOUR FOR BACKSTITCHING
Backstitch all outlines using 3799.

KEY

208 Flower petals

310 Summer house on hill, swan's faces

311 Pale areas on cushion

317 Birds' wings

336 Mid-toned areas on cushion

469 Fields at top right

470 Dark areas of grass

471 Pale areas of grass

597 Dark areas of sash and ribbon on hat

598 Mid-toned areas of sash and ribbon on hat

712 Pages of book, and bird's breast

721 Swans' beaks

762 Dark areas of swans' feathers

762/White Mid-toned areas of swans' feathers

813 Dark areas of water

823 Dark areas of cushion

827 Mid-toned areas of water

828 Pale areas of water

937 Leaves of bulrushes, central bush at top left and dark areas of fields at top right

938 Pale areas of hair, and bulrushes

948 Pale areas of dress

951 Dark areas of face and hands

3341 Very dark areas of dress and hat

3347 Bushes at top left

3371 Dark areas of hair

3770 Pale areas of face and hands

3811 Pale areas of sash and ribbon on hat

3824 Mid-toned areas of dress and hat

White Pale areas of swans' feathers

A tranquil lakeside scene in summer

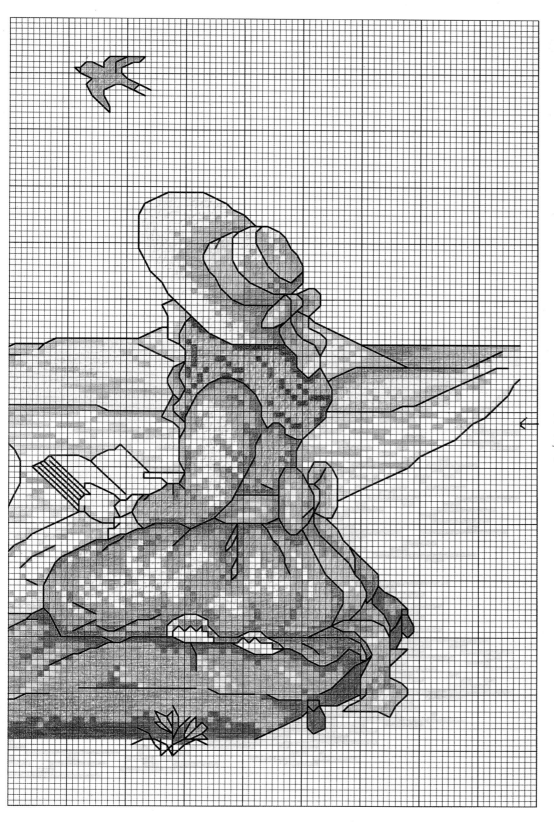

Refer to page 31 for the key to this chart

By the Fireside

This is a typical turn-of-the-century fireplace with cast iron bars and decorative tiles, and the ever-present dogs on the mantelpiece. This nostalgic picture would look lovely in the living room.

ACTUAL DESIGN SIZE
12 x 9½in (30 x 24cm)

MATERIALS
● 1 piece of 14-count Aida in white measuring approximately 17 x 14¼in (42.5 x 36cm)
● No 24 tapestry needle

INSTRUCTIONS
Mark the centre of the chart. Find the centre of your fabric and make long tacking stitches across and down. Using two strands of stranded cotton (except for backstitching where you use one strand only) begin your work following the chart. To stitch the reflection of the dogs, use one strand of thread and work the first half of the cross stitch in black for the dogs' ears and ecru for the bodies, then complete the cross stitches using a single strand of sky blue. For full instructions for cross stitches, backstitches and special shaping stitches see the *Techniques* section on pages 121-126 of this book.

THREADS

DMC Colour	Metres
304 cranberry	2
310 black	8
347 dark strawberry pink	1
367 mid green	1
413 dark grey	1
414 pewter	2
415 grey	5
434 brown	1
435 dark caramel	1
437 fudge brown	1
470 green	1
471 light olive green	1
472 light moss green	1
676 pale mustard	2
677 pale yellow	21
680 French mustard	1
720 tan	1
725 dark yellow	1
729 dark mustard	1
739 ivory	2
762 silver grey	2
797 deep blue	1
798 light royal blue	1
800 forget-me-not blue	4
809 blue	1
832 bronze	2
833 light bronze	2
977 cinnamon	1
3371 dark chocolate brown	1
3706 coral pink	1
3708 light coral pink	1
3823 pale banana yellow	3
Ecru	3

COLOUR FOR BACKSTITCHING
Backstitch all outlines using 310.

KEY

- 304 Flower petals
- 310 Patches, eyes and nose on dogs, flower centres, tile surrounds, coal, dark area of grate
- 347 Rim of pink shoes
- 367 Leaves
- 413 Shading on grate
- 414 Mid-toned grey on grate, dark shading on chimney hood
- 415 Pale areas on grate, mid-toned shading on chimney hood, tile surrounds
- 434 Dark areas on brown shoe uppers
- 435 Main areas on brown shoes
- 437 Mid-toned areas on chimney, shading on upper part of brown shoes
- 470 Dark area on green shoe on right
- 471 Green shoes
- 472 Bows on green shoes
- 676 Upper part of brown shoes, shading on chimney
- 677 Main area of fireplace
- 680 Shadow in chimney
- 720 Red tips of flames
- 725 Yellow part of flames

The household's shoes are warming in front of the blazing fire

- 729 Main shading on chimney
- 739 Palest area on chimney
- 762 Highlight on chimney
- 797 Dark areas of bows of blue shoes
- 798 Backs and bows of blue shoes
- 800 Mirror glass
- 809 Blue shoes
- 832 Fireguard rail, inner rim of mirror frame
- 833 Outer part of mirror frame
- 977 Mid-toned areas of flames
- 3371 Heel of brown shoe
- 3706 Backs and dark areas of straps of pink shoes
- 3708 Pink shoes
- 3823 Tile backgrounds
- Ecru Dogs

An Evergreen Garland

This very simple wreath makes a charming decoration for a wooden trinket box. The metallic gold thread used in the stitching catches the light and sparkles beautifully. If you prefer, you can use the stitched design to make a decorative Christmas card. For a set of cards, ring the changes by alternating silver thread with gold.

ACTUAL DESIGN SIZE
1¾ x 2¼in (4.5 x 5.5cm)

MATERIALS
● 1 piece of 18-count Aida in cream measuring approximately 6½ x 7in (16.5 x 17.5cm)
● No 24 tapestry needle
● A wooden needle box

INSTRUCTIONS
Mark the centre of the chart. Find the centre of your fabric and make long tacking stitches across and down. Using two strands of stranded cotton (except for backstitching where you use one strand only) begin your work following the chart. For full instructions for cross stitches, backstitches and special shaping stitches see the *Techniques* section on pages 121-126 of this book. If desired, insert the stitched piece into a needle box, following the manufacturer's instructions.

THREADS

DMC Colour	Metres
321 crimson	1
904 pale green	2
3799 charcoal grey	1
5284 metallic gold	1

COLOURS FOR BACKSTITCHING
Backstitch the garland and ribbon bow using 3799.
Backstitch the gold baubles using 5284.

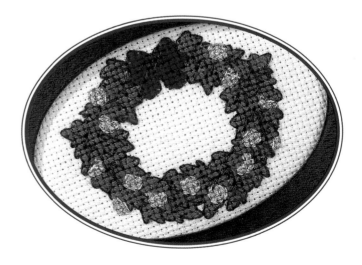

The metallic gold stitches twinkle like baubles on a real wreath

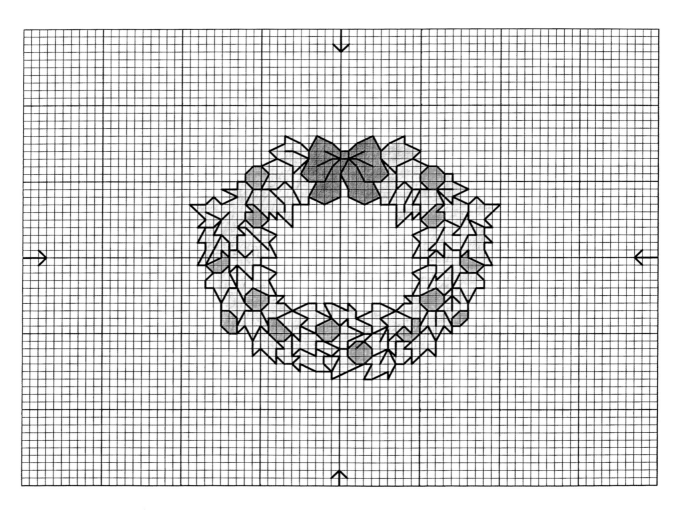

KEY

■ 321 Ribbon bow

▦ 904 Leaves

▩ 5284 Baubles

An Easter Surprise

This cross-stitched Easter egg was based on a beautiful enamel egg which was given to me by my husband. The egg stands on a gold ring and opens up to reveal a hollow centre in which can be stored special trinkets. This design would make a particularly lovely Easter card, perhaps for a nephew or niece. If you prefer, you could make the design into a framed picture.

ACTUAL DESIGN SIZE

3¼ x 2in (8 x 5cm)

MATERIALS

- 1 piece of 18-count linen in white measuring approximately 8 x 6¾in (20 x 17cm)
- No 24 tapestry needle
- Gift card (optional)

INSTRUCTIONS

Mark the centre of the chart. Find the centre of your fabric and make long tacking stitches across and down. Using two strands of stranded cotton (except for backstitching where you use one strand only) begin your work following the chart. For full instructions for cross stitches, backstitches and special shaping stitches see the *Techniques* section on pages 121-126 of this book.

THREADS

DMC Colour	Metres
745 yellow	1
796 royal blue	3
3705 dark pink	1
3706 pink	1
5269 metallic green	1
5284 metallic gold	3

COLOUR FOR BACKSTITCHING

Backstitch the flower detail and the egg using 5284.

KEY

- 745 Flower centres
- 796 Background of egg
- 3705 Dark areas of flower petals
- 3706 Pale areas of flower petals
- 5269 Leaves
- 5284 Base of egg

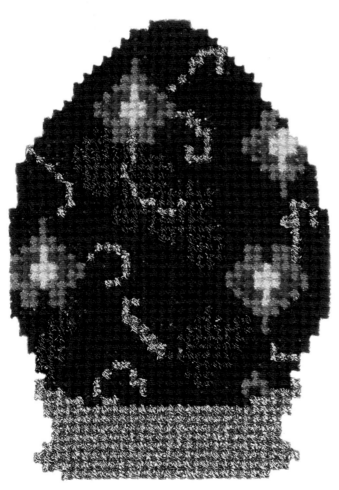

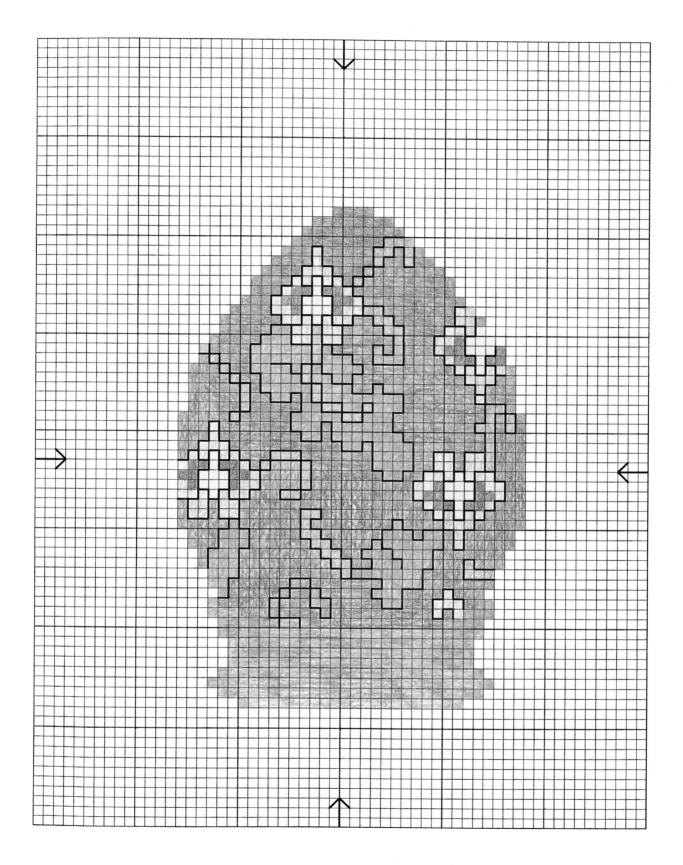

Learning the ABC

With this soft and pretty alphabet you can stitch a child's name or initials to sew onto clothing or bedlinen. Another idea might be to make a door plate with a child's name on it. Simply stretch the finished embroidery on to backing board and put it in a plain frame.

ACTUAL DESIGN SIZE (OF 'EMMA')
2 x 9¼in (5 x 23cm)

MATERIALS (USED IN 'EMMA')
- 1 piece of 18-count white linen measuring approximately 6¾ x 14in (17 x 35cm)
- No 24 tapestry needle

INSTRUCTIONS
Mark the centre of the chart. Find the centre of your fabric and make long tacking stitches across and down. Using two strands of stranded cotton (except for backstitching where you use one strand only) begin your work following the chart. For full instructions for cross stitches, backstitches and special shaping stitches see the *Techniques* section on pages 121-126.

THREADS

DMC Colour	Metres for each letter
792 dark mauve	1
794 pale mauve	1
961 dark pink	1
963 pink	1
986 dark green	1
988 light forest green	1

COLOURS FOR BACKSTITCHING
Backstitch the flowers and stamens using 961.
Backstitch the leaves using 986.

Pretty blossom flowers and delicate green leaves decorate these initials

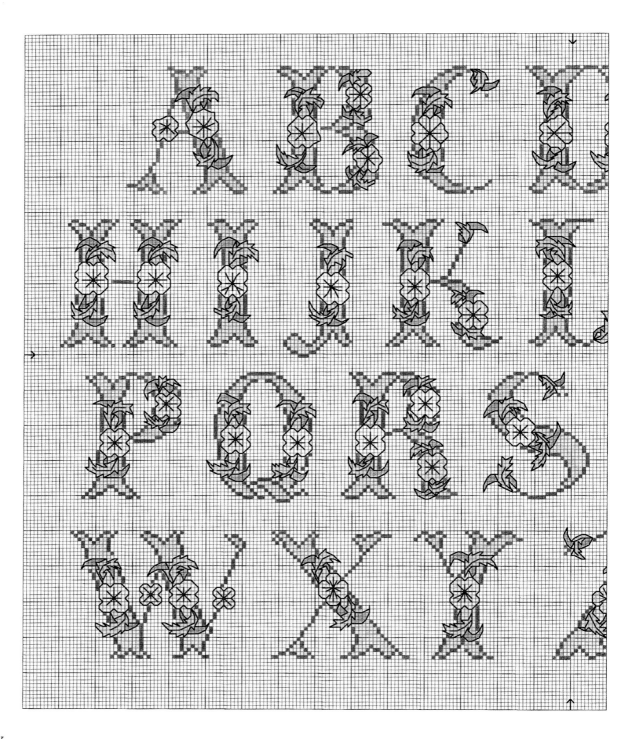

KEY

▓	792 Dark areas of letters		▦	963 Flowers
▦	794 Pale areas of letters		▦	986 Dark leaves

You can personalize clothes, bedlinen and even bags with these stitched letters

988 Pale leaves

Baby's Birth Sampler

This is a beautiful Victorian-style birth sampler stitched in the traditional colours of the era using khaki-coloured linen and soft, gentle shades for the embroidery threads. If you prefer, you can make the sampler more contemporary to suit the colour scheme of your interior by substituting colours of your choice.

ACTUAL DESIGN SIZE
15¼ x 16in (38 x 40cm)

MATERIALS
● 1 piece of 16-count linen in natural measuring approximately 20 x 20¾in (50 x 52cm)
● No 24 tapestry needle

INSTRUCTIONS
Mark the centre of the chart. Find the centre of your fabric and make long tacking stitches across and down. Using two strands of stranded cotton (except for backstitching

Stitch this rocking horse motif to make a charming greetings card

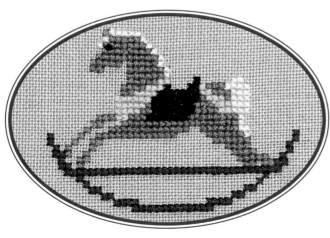

where you use one strand only) begin your work following the chart. For full instructions for cross stitches, backstitches and special shaping stitches see the *Techniques* section on pages 121-126 of this book.

THREADS

DMC Colour	Metres
310 black	1
334 light blue	3
347 dark pink	10
434 brown	2
677 pale yellow	2
746 cream	4
938 dark brown	1
3345 dark green	3
3712 pink	2
3808 dark petrol blue	5
3809 petrol blue	6
3820 dark yellow	1

COLOUR FOR BACKSTITCHING
Backstitch the legs and detail on the crib using 434.

FRENCH KNOTS
For the eyes on the brown horse use 310.
For the eyes on the black horse use 434.

KEY

■ 310 Outer rocking horses' saddles

▦ 334 Flowers in central row, central rules

▦ 347 Flowers in central row, sampler edging

▦ 434 Outer rocking horses

▦ 677 Cribs, rocking horses' tails, flower centres in top row

▦ 746 Crib hoods, alternate flowers in top row, central numbers in bottom row

■ 938 Rocking horse rockers

▦ 3345 Foliage in top and centre rows, rules at bottom

▦ 3712 Alternate flowers in top row, first set of numbers in bottom row

▦ 3808 Capital letters of alphabet

▦ 3809 Lower case letters of alphabet, writing in lower half of sampler, last set of numbers in bottom row

▦ 3820 Rocking horses' decorative tack

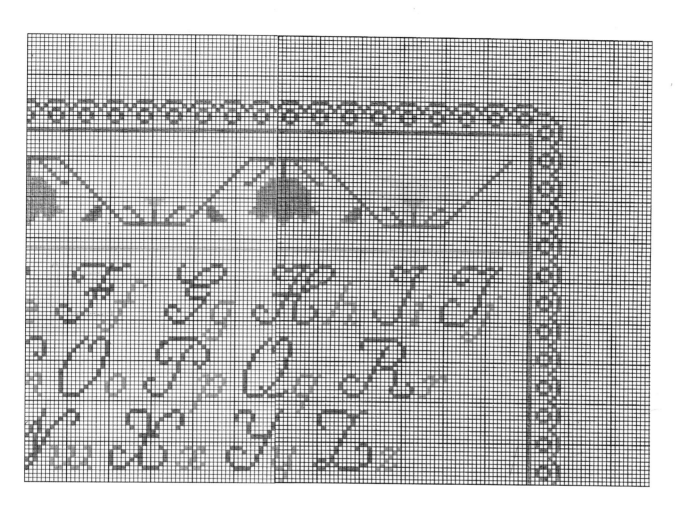

Page 50	Page 51
Page 52	Page 53

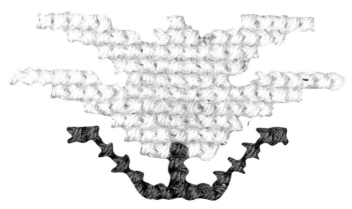

The chart is split over four pages: page 50 shows the top left, page 51 the top right, page 52 the bottom left and page 53 the bottom right

This traditional flower border design is used to separate the different sections of the sampler

Rockabye Horse

Last Christmas, I was given a delightful wooden rocking horse, which gave me the inspiration for this lovely design. Using only four colours of embroidery thread, this rocking horse is very quickly stitched and would make a lovely addition to the nursery, either as a picture or as a box lid.

ACTUAL DESIGN SIZE
3½ x 4¾in (9 x 12cm)

MATERIALS
- 1 piece of 18-count Aida in white measuring approximately 8¼ x 9½in (20.5 x 24cm)
- No 24 tapestry needle

INSTRUCTIONS
Mark the centre of the chart. Find the centre of your fabric and make long tacking stitches across and down. Using two strands of stranded cotton (except for backstitching where you use one strand of cotton only)

begin your work following the chart. For full instructions for cross stitches, backstitches and special shaping stitches see the *Techniques* section on pages 121-126 of this book.

THREADS

DMC Colour	Metres
282 metallic gold	4
310 black	3
434 brown	1
712 light cream	2

COLOUR FOR BACKSTITCHING
Backstitch the stirrup using 282.

With its glittering reins, bridle and shining rocker, this rocking horse is every child's ride to wonderland. You can stitch the design as a picture, a greetings card, or as a pretty trinket box lid

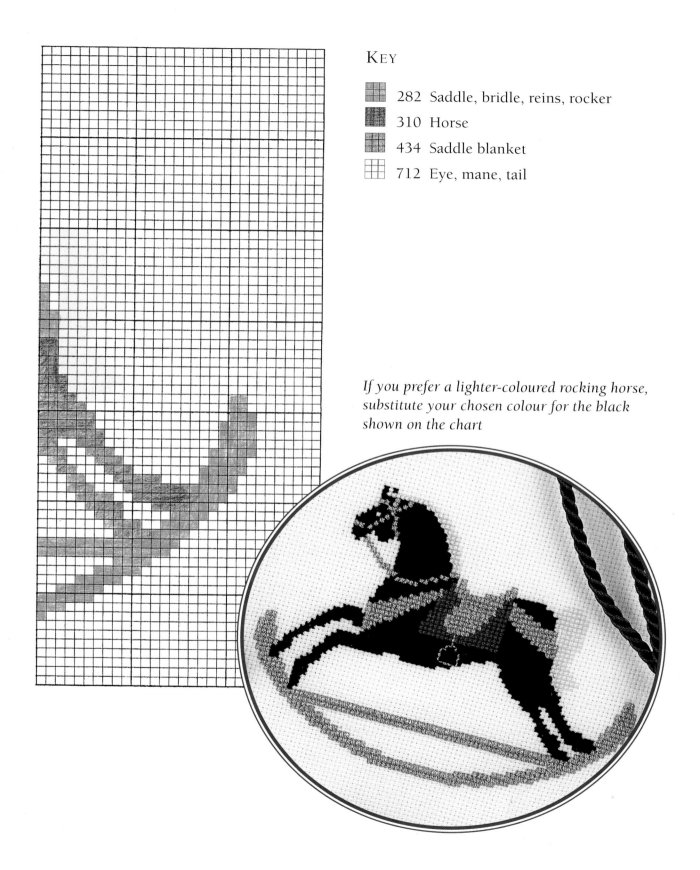

KEY

282 Saddle, bridle, reins, rocker
310 Horse
434 Saddle blanket
712 Eye, mane, tail

If you prefer a lighter-coloured rocking horse, substitute your chosen colour for the black shown on the chart

A Window full of Dolls

These five dolls, with their elegant dresses and pretty hats, are typical of the fine porcelain dolls that were made a hundred years ago. This is a challenging design for an experienced stitcher as, in addition to cross stitch, it involves petit point for the fine detail of the dolls' faces.

ACTUAL DESIGN SIZE
9½ x 13in (24 x 32.5cm)

MATERIALS
● 1 piece of 18-count linen in cream measuring approximately 14¼ x 18in (36 x 45cm)
● No 24 tapestry needle

INSTRUCTIONS
Mark the centre of the chart. Find the centre of your fabric and make long tacking stitches across and down. Using two strands of stranded cotton (except for backstitching, long stitches, lazy daisy stitches and the blue background of the window, where you use one strand only) begin your work following the chart. Work the faces of the dolls in petit point, following the individual charts. For full instructions for cross stitches, backstitches, special shaping stitches and petit point see the *Techniques* section on pages 121-126 of this book.

THREADS

DMC Colour	Metres
300 chestnut	3
310 black	2
318 dark grey	1
336 dark blue	1
356 light russet	1
436 caramel	2
469 olive green	3
470 green	1
676 pale mustard	2
677 pale yellow	1
712 light cream	1
729 dark mustard	1
738 beige	1
739 ivory	3
744 yellow	4
745 dark straw yellow	9
762 silver grey	9
798 royal blue	4
799 cornflower blue	8
800 forget-me-not blue	1
809 blue	3
823 navy blue	1
830 dark taupe	1
920 dark cinnamon	1
921 nutmeg brown	1
937 sage green	2
945 blush pink	1
950 dark oyster	1
951 flesh pink	2
975 dark ginger	1
3325 powder blue	1
3347 moss green	1
3371 dark brown	2
3685 dark plum	1
3687 light plum	2
3770 flesh	2
3773 mink	1
3774 oyster	1
3799 charcoal	3
3803 plum	4
3823 dark cream	2
5284 metallic gold	1
White	3

COLOURS FOR BACKSTITCHING
Backstitch the hair of the brunette doll using 300.
Backstitch the detail of the window and woodwork using 436.
Backstitch the hair on the blonde dolls using 729.
Backstitch the hair on the red-headed doll using 920.

LONG STITCH

Use a single strand for all long stitches.

For the tassel detail of the cushion use 823.

For the feather detail of the green hat use 920.

For the end detail of the plaits use 3371.

For the ribbon ends of the doll's plaits use white.

For the hair ribbon on the left-hand side doll use 799.

LAZY DAISY STITCH

For the bows of the plaits use a single strand of white and 799.

FRENCH KNOTS

For the dolls' pupils use 3799.

Fine stitching emphasizes the features of this doll's face

KEY (CROSS STITCH)

300 Dark areas of hair of doll on right, dark areas of brown dress

310 Soles of shoes

318 Dark areas of petticoat, collar and cuff of doll on right, dark areas of bonnet and ribbon, pale area on shoe sole of doll with plaits

336 Light areas of window seat

469 Mid-toned areas of dress and hat of doll wearing green

470 Pale areas of dress and hat of doll wearing green

676 Dark areas of hair of doll on left and of small doll in centre

677 Light areas of hair of doll on left and of small doll in centre

712 Light areas of dress of small doll in centre

738 Dark areas of dress of doll in centre

739 Mid-toned areas of dress of small doll in centre

744 Dark areas of dress of doll on right

745 Mid-toned areas of dress on doll on right, neckband and waistband on dress of doll on left

762 Mid-toned areas of petticoat, collar and cuff of doll on right, mid-toned areas of hat and ribbon of doll with plaits, dark areas of cuffs of doll on left

762/White Pale areas of petticoat, collar and cuff of doll on right, pale areas of hat and ribbon of doll with plaits, and pale areas of cuffs of doll on left

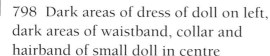 798 Dark areas of dress of doll on left, dark areas of waistband, collar and hairband of small doll in centre

799 Mid-toned areas of dress of doll on left

800 Window

809 Pale areas of dress of doll on left, pale areas of waistband, collar and hairband of small doll in centre

823 Dark areas of window seat

920 Dark areas of hair of doll wearing green

921 Pale areas of hair of doll wearing green

937 Dark areas of dress and hat of doll wearing green

951 Dark shading on arms

975 Light areas of hair of doll on right

3371 Hair of doll with plaits

3685 Dark areas on dress of doll with plaits

3687 Light areas on dress of doll with plaits

3770 Arms

3803 Mid-toned areas on dress of doll with plaits

3823 Pale areas of dress of doll on right

5284 Neck brooch of doll wearing green

White Pattern at base of petticoat of doll on right

Refer to pages 60-61 for the key to this chart

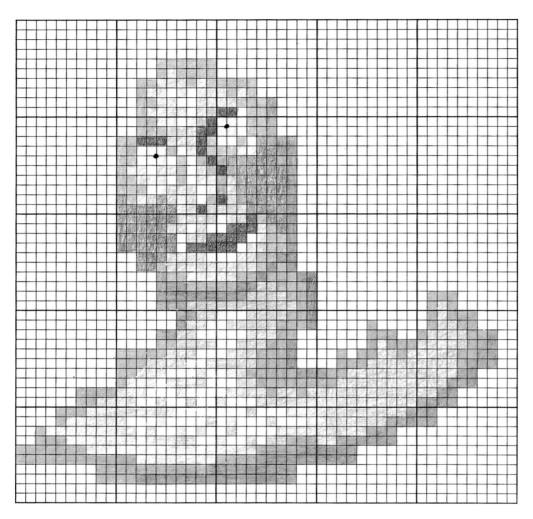

This doll has her hair arranged in ringlets, a popular style in years gone by

KEY (PETIT POINT)

300 Eyebrows of doll wearing green, shading around eyes on doll on left

356 Lips

676 Eyebrows of small doll in centre

830 Eyes of doll with plaits

920 Shading on neck

945 Cheeks

950 Shading on neck

951 Mid-toned areas on face and neck

3325 Eyes of doll on left, in centre and on right

3347 Eyes of doll wearing green

3371 Eyebrows of doll with plaits

3770 Pale areas on face and neck

3773 Eyelids of doll wearing green

3774 Medium shading on face and neck

White Eyes

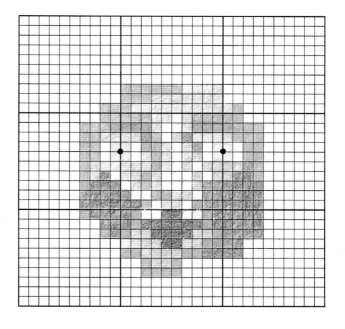

This demure doll is wearing a traditional sash around her waist

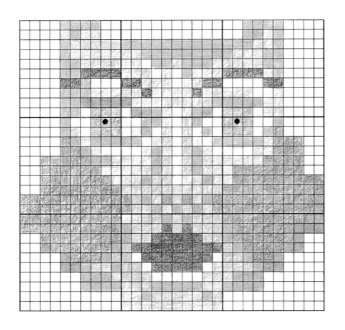

A large frilled bonnet keeps this doll's hair in check

This flame-haired beauty sports decorative feathers in her hat

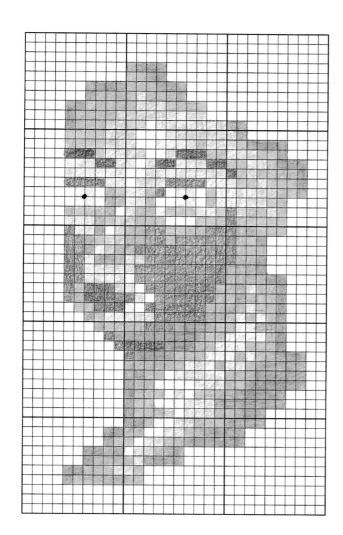

This severe-faced doll presides over her colleagues on the window seat

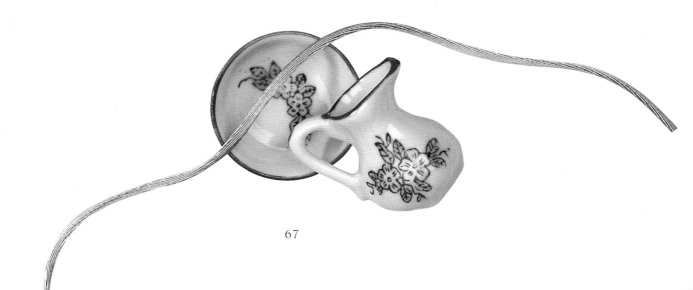

The Dolls' Tea Party

This delightful nursery scene is typical of the early 1900s, with the dolls' house, spinning top, teddy bear, building blocks and pretty china tea set.

ACTUAL DESIGN SIZE
8¼ x 7¼in (21 x 18.5cm)

MATERIALS
● 1 piece of 18-count Aida in white measuring approximately 13¼ x 12in (33 x 30cm)
● No 24 tapestry needle

INSTRUCTIONS
Mark the centre of the chart. Find the centre of your fabric and make long tacking stitches across and down. Using two strands of stranded cotton (except for backstitching where you use one strand only) begin your work following the chart. For full instructions for cross stitches, backstitches and special shaping stitches see the *Techniques* section on pages 121-126 of this book.

THREADS

DMC Colour	Metres
310 black	1
312 dark blue	2
322 blue	4
334 light blue	1
347 dark pink	4
420 toffee brown	2
433 light brown	3
434 brown	1
435 caramel	1
676 mustard	1
677 pale yellow	4
742 pale orange	1
744 yellow	1
746 cream	5
754 flesh	1
762 light grey	3
801 dark brown	5
918 dark terracotta	1
919 terracotta	1
938 chocolate brown	2
3325 powder blue	1
3328 pink	6
3347 dark green	2
3348 green	5
3371 dark chocolate brown	2
3712 dusky pink	3
3774 pale flesh	1
3828 mink	2
5284 metallic gold	1
White	4

COLOURS FOR BACKSTITCHING
Backstitch the A and Z building bricks using 312.
Backstitch the E building brick using 347.
Backstitch the J building brick using 918.
Backstitch all other outlines using 3371.

Key

 310 Girl's shoe

312 Dark areas of dress and spinning top

322 Mid-toned areas of dress and spinning top, shorts, shoes and ribbon on hat of doll, dark areas on crockery

334 Pale areas on dress, spinning top and crockery, doll's shirt and stockings, girl's eyes

347 Dolls' house curtains, rug edging, dark areas on curtains, cushion and tablecloth edging

420 Dark areas of teddy

433 Building blocks

434 Top of skirting and picture rail

435 Skirting board

676 Markings and mane on giraffe, hair of girl and doll

677 Giraffe, biscuits, dolls' house walls, doll's hat

742 Flower centres on tablecloth

744 Flowers on tablecloth

746 Tablecloth

754 Girl's cheeks

762 Dark areas of girl's apron, bonnet and stockings

762/White Mid-toned areas of girl's apron, bonnet and stockings

801 Chair

918 Dark part of dolls' house roof

919 Light part of dolls' house roof

938 Football, dark areas of chair

3325 Sky

3328 Mid-toned areas of curtain, cushion and tablecloth edging

3347 Dark areas of rug

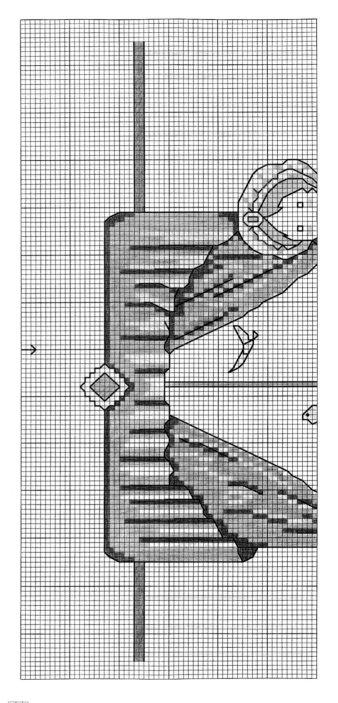

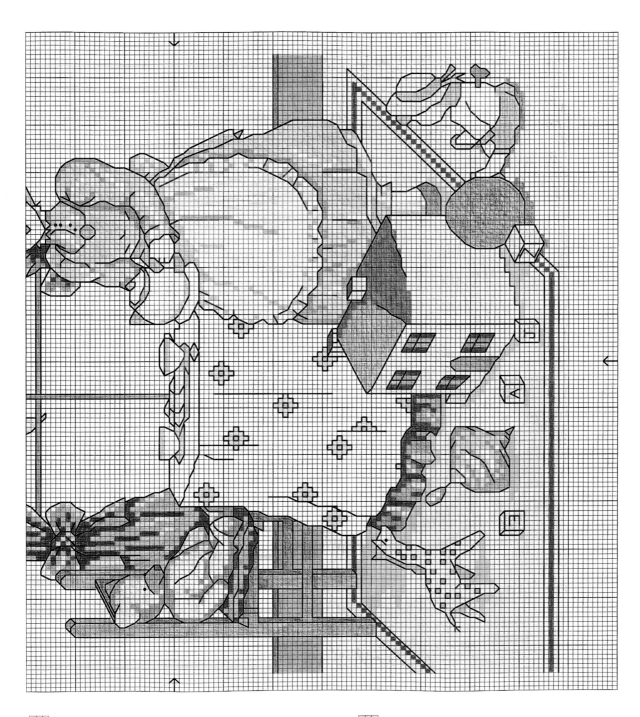

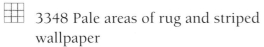 3348 Pale areas of rug and striped wallpaper

3712 Light areas of curtain, cushion and tablecloth edging

3774 Face and hands of girl and doll

 3828 Birds

5284 Brooch on girl's dress

White Pale areas of girl's apron, bonnet and stockings

A Skaters' Waltz

No book on nostalgic cross-stitch designs would be complete without a reference to this enjoyable winter pastime. In this evocative scene, two figures skate on a frozen lake, well muffled against the cold. The bright colouring on the clothing attracts attention and the fur and folds are delicately rendered.

ACTUAL DESIGN SIZE
11½ x 8¼in (29 x 21cm)

MATERIALS
● 1 piece of 16-count Aida in white measuring approximately 16 x 13in (40 x 32.5cm)
● No 24 tapestry needle

INSTRUCTIONS
Mark the centre of the chart. Find the centre of your fabric and make long tacking stitches across and down. Using two strands of stranded cotton (except for backstitching where you use one strand only) begin your work following the chart. For full instructions for cross stitches, backstitches and special shaping stitches see the *Techniques* section on pages 123-127 of this book.

This girl's cheeks are aglow with the frosty cold

THREADS

DMC Colour	Metres
300 chestnut	1
310 black	2
415 grey	2
433 brown	2
434 light brown	1
676 mustard	1
677 pale yellow	1
746 cream	1
760 pink	2
761 pale pink	2
762 silver grey	7
796 royal blue	6
797 deep blue	1
798 blue	1
820 midnight blue	1
898 dark brown	3
951 flesh pink	1
3712 strawberry pink	2
3755 smoky blue	1
3770 flesh	2
3799 charcoal grey	6
3790 khaki brown	2
White	13

COLOURS FOR BACKSTITCHING
Backstitch the skates using 310.
Backstitch all other outlines using 3799.

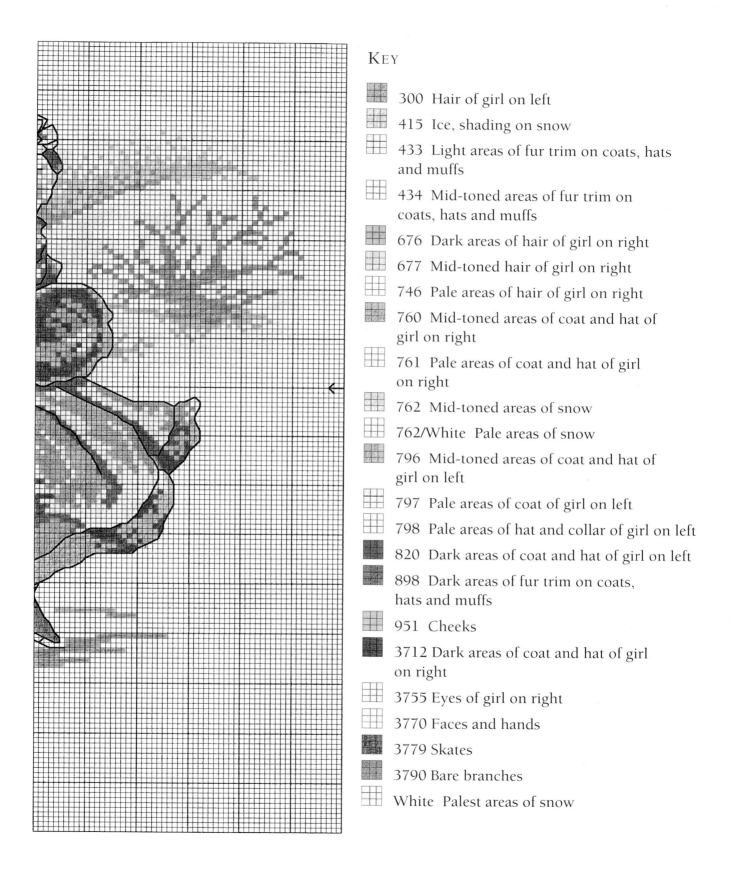

KEY

300 Hair of girl on left

415 Ice, shading on snow

433 Light areas of fur trim on coats, hats and muffs

434 Mid-toned areas of fur trim on coats, hats and muffs

676 Dark areas of hair of girl on right

677 Mid-toned hair of girl on right

746 Pale areas of hair of girl on right

760 Mid-toned areas of coat and hat of girl on right

761 Pale areas of coat and hat of girl on right

762 Mid-toned areas of snow

762/White Pale areas of snow

796 Mid-toned areas of coat and hat of girl on left

797 Pale areas of coat of girl on left

798 Pale areas of hat and collar of girl on left

820 Dark areas of coat and hat of girl on left

898 Dark areas of fur trim on coats, hats and muffs

951 Cheeks

3712 Dark areas of coat and hat of girl on right

3755 Eyes of girl on right

3770 Faces and hands

3779 Skates

3790 Bare branches

White Palest areas of snow

Sunday Best Hat

With its gorgeous feathers, flowers and plumes, this hat certainly demands attention; a hat to be worn when you want to turn heads. The stitched picture would look lovely on a bedroom wall, adding a touch of nostalgic glamour and sophistication, and warming the room with its rich red tones.

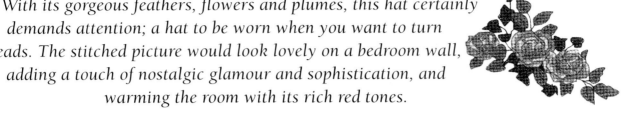

ACTUAL DESIGN SIZE
9¼ x 6½in (23 x 16.5cm)

MATERIALS
● 1 piece of 18-count Aida in cream measuring approximately 14 x 11¼in (35 x 28cm)
● No 24 tapestry needle

INSTRUCTIONS
Mark the centre of the chart. Find the centre of your fabric and make long tacking stitches across and down. Using two strands of stranded cotton (except for backstitching where you use one strand only) begin your work following the chart. For full instructions for cross stitches, backstitches and special shaping stitches see the *Techniques* section on pages 121-126 of this book.

THREADS

DMC Colour	Metres
319 bottle green	1
676 pale mustard	2
677 pale yellow	4
729 mustard	1
746 cream	6
760 pink	5
814 burgundy	6
815 claret	5
816 maroon	4
890 dark green	1
3328 dark raspberry	2
3345 dark ivy green	1
3346 ivy green	1
3712 strawberry pink	3
3713 pale pink	5

COLOURS FOR BACKSTITCHING
Backstitch the straw hat rim and inside detail using 729.
Backstitch the hat feathers using 760.
Backstitch the detail of the hat, ribbon, tufty feather and top left of hat using 814.
Backstitch the ivy leaves and stems using 890.
Backstitch the rose leaves and stems using 3345.
Backstitch the roses, bow and box stripes using 3328.

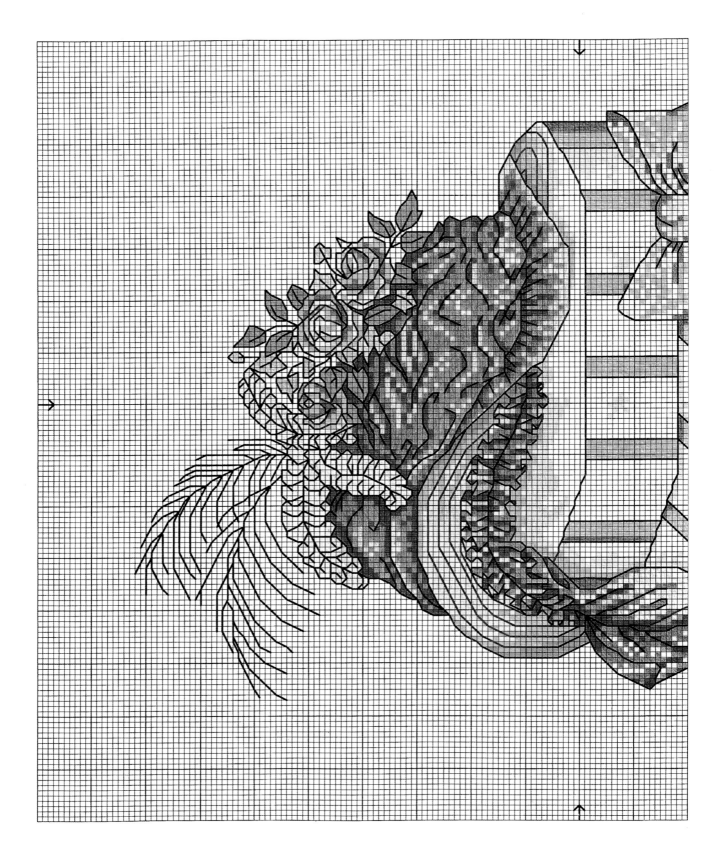

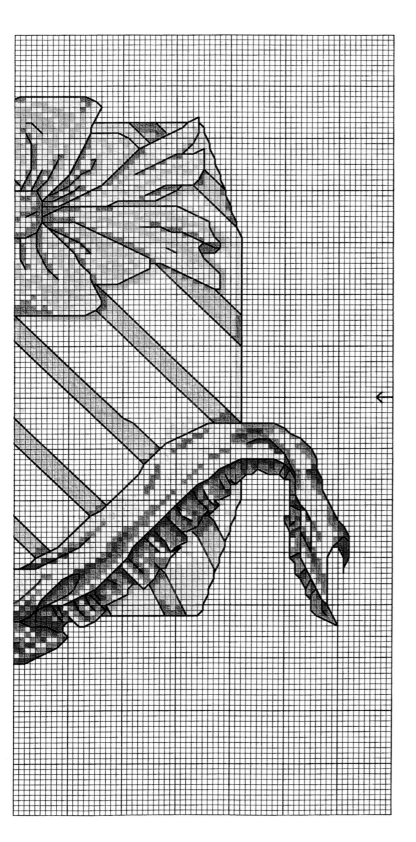

KEY

	319	Pale leaves
	676	Dark areas of hat box, mid-toned areas of underside of hat
	677	Mid-toned areas of hat box, pale areas of underside of hat
	729	Shading on top right of hat box, and on underside of hat
	746	Pale areas of hat box
	760	Mid-toned areas of ribbon and stripes on hat box, mid-toned areas of rose petals
	814	Dark areas of hat and ribbon
	815	Mid-toned areas of hat and ribbon
	816	Light areas of hat and ribbon
	3346	Dark leaves
	3712	Dark areas of ribbon and stripes on hat box, dark areas of rose petals
	3713	Pale areas of ribbon on hat box, pale areas of rose petals, feather

A Sunday hat with exquisite style

Dancing Days

This dainty shoe and twirling ribbon were the epitome of turn-of-the-century style, when dressing up really meant putting on the finery: dancing shoes and hair ribbons were essential items of dress. Stitch this pretty greetings card for a touch of old-fashioned glamour.

ACTUAL DESIGN SIZE
3 x 3½in (7.5 x 9cm)

MATERIALS
- 1 piece of 18-count Aida in cream measuring approximately 7 x 8in (17.5 x 20cm)
- No 24 tapestry needle
- Gift card and envelope (optional)

INSTRUCTIONS
Mark the centre of the chart. Find the centre of your fabric and make long tacking stitches across and down. Using two strands of stranded cotton (except for backstitching where you use one strand only) begin your work following the chart. For full instructions for cross stitches, backstitches, special shaping stitches, long stitches and French knots, see the *Techniques* section on pages 121-126 of this book.

THREADS

DMC Colour	Metres
597 turquoise	2
598 pale turquoise	1
744 yellow	2
3808 petrol blue	1
3810 dark turquoise	2
3811 aqua	1
5284 metallic gold	1

COLOURS FOR BACKSTITCHING
Backstitch the ribbon and the ribbon on the shoe using 3808.
Backstitch the shoe using 744.

FRENCH KNOTS
For the edging on the shoe use 3808.

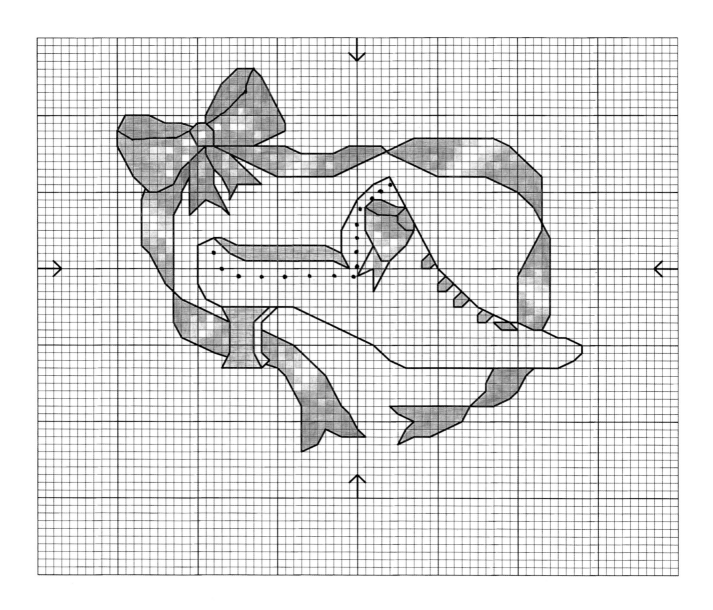

KEY

 597 Mid-toned shading on ribbon

598 Light areas on ribbon

744 Shoe

3810 Dark shading on ribbon

3811 Pale areas of ribbon

5284 Heel and inside of shoe

Decked with Flowers

Spring is certainly in the air with this pretty greetings card. The fresh flowers entwined around the hat are emphasized by the bottle green card. You can use another colour of card if you prefer, but try to match one of the colours used in the stitching.

83

ACTUAL DESIGN SIZE
2½ x 3½in (6.5 x 9cm)

MATERIALS
● 1 piece of 18-count Aida in cream
measuring approximately 6 x 8in
(15 x 20cm)
● No 24 tapestry needle
● Gift card and envelope (optional)

INSTRUCTIONS
Mark the centre of the chart. Find the centre
of your fabric and make long tacking stitches
across and down. Using two strands of
stranded cotton (except for backstitching
where you use one strand only) begin your
work following the chart. For full
instructions for cross stitches, backstitches,
special shaping stitches, long stitches and
French knots see the *Techniques* section on
pages 121-126 of this book.

THREADS

DMC Colour	Metres
309 deep pink	1
321 crimson	1
743 yellow	1
745 pale yellow	3
819 very pale pink	2
899 pink	1
963 light pink	2
986 dark green	1
987 green	1
989 pale green	1

COLOURS FOR BACKSTITCHING
Backstitch the flowers using 309.
Backstitch the leaves using 987.
Backstitch the hat using 745.

LONG STITCHES
For the centres of the star flowers use 309.
For the lines in the tulips use 309.
For the veins of the leaves use 986.
For the stalks on the tulips and the hat use
two strands of 986.

FRENCH KNOTS
For the centres of the star flowers use 309.

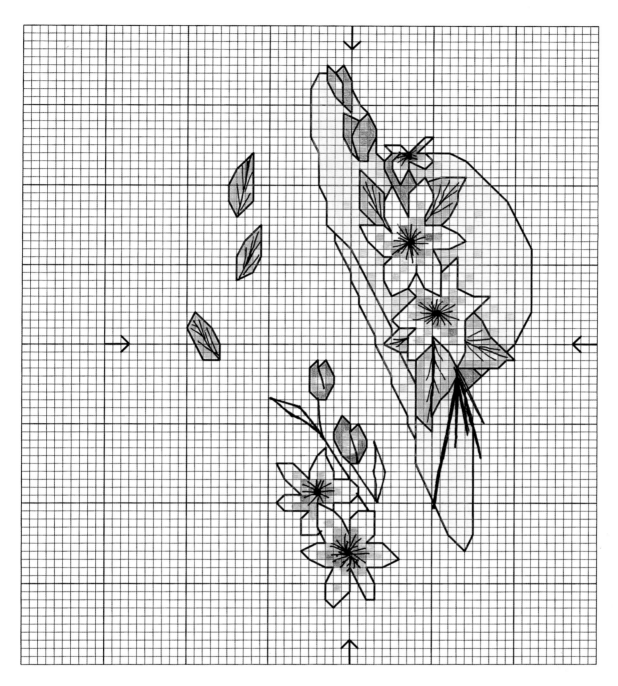

KEY

321 Hat band

743 Shading on hat

745 Hat

819 Pale areas of petals

899 Dark areas of petals

963 Mid-toned areas of petals

987 Dark areas of leaves

989 Pale areas of leaves

Pedal Pushing

This unusual project was great fun to design, and the use of just two colours proved very effective. A hundred years ago it must have been a familiar sight to see women, both young and old, cycling along the street, with dresses billowing and fancy hats flying off in the wind! Frame this picture in black for best effect.

ACTUAL DESIGN SIZE
5 x 2¼in (12.5 x 5.5cm)

MATERIALS
- 1 piece of 16-count linen in white measuring approximately 10 x 7in (25 x 17.5cm)
- No 24 tapestry needle
- Flexihoop (optional)

INSTRUCTIONS
Mark the centre of the chart. Find the centre of your fabric and make long tacking stitches across and down. Using two strands of stranded cotton (except for backstitching where you use one strand only) begin your work following the chart. For full instructions for cross stitches, backstitches and special shaping stitches see the *Techniques* section on pages 121-126 of this book.

THREADS

DMC Colour	Metres
310 black	2
3799 charcoal grey	5

COLOUR FOR BACKSTITCHING
Backstitch all outlines using 310.

LONG STITCH
For the bicycle spokes use 310.

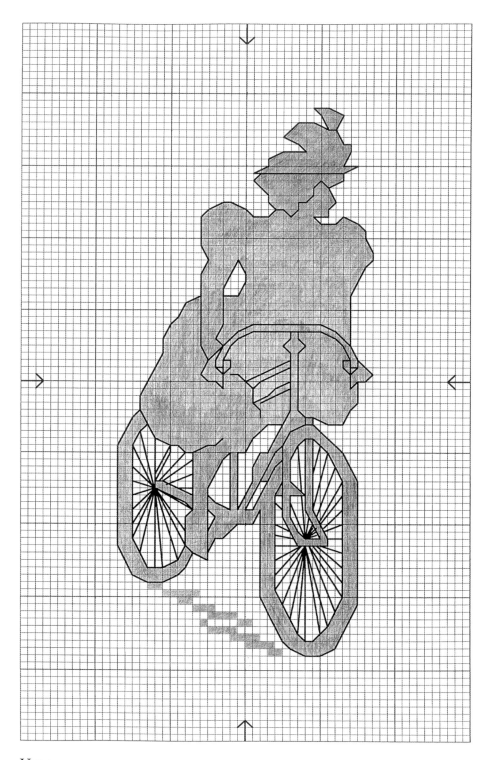

KEY

3799 Lady, bicycle and shadow

Afternoon Promenade

This elegant hat sports feathers and leaves for decoration, both of which were popular fashion accessories in the 1900s. You can stitch this design either for a trinket box lid or for a greetings card.

ACTUAL DESIGN SIZE
2¼ x 3in (5.5 x 7.5cm)

MATERIALS
● 1 piece of 18-count linen in white measuring approximately 7 x 8in (17.5 x 20cm)
● No 24 tapestry needle
● Ceramic trinket box (optional)

INSTRUCTIONS
Mark the centre of the chart. Find the centre of your fabric and make long tacking stitches across and down. Using two strands of stranded cotton (except for backstitching where you use one strand only) begin your work following the chart. For full instructions for cross stitches, backstitches and special shaping stitches see the *Techniques* section on pages 121-126 of this book.

THREADS

DMC Colour	Metres
310 black	1
350 red	1
353 pink	1
413 grey	1
742 pale orange	1
744 dark yellow	1
745 yellow	1
746 cream	1
904 green	1
905 lime green	2
948 pale salmon pink	2
3345 dark green	1
3799 charcoal grey	1

COLOURS FOR BACKSTITCHING
Backstitch the feathers and detail using 742. **Backstitch the flower petals** using 350. **Backstitch the leaf veins** using 3345. **Backstitch the hat and remaining outlines** using 310.

LONG STITCH
For the stamens use 744.

Just the hat to wear when taking the air for an afternoon promenade

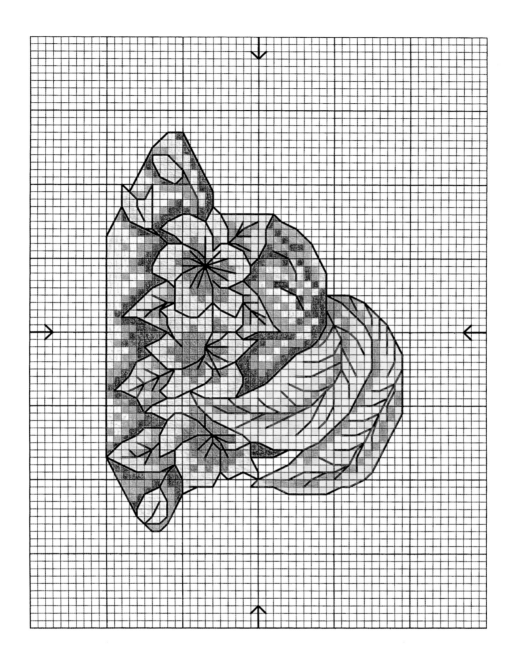

KEY

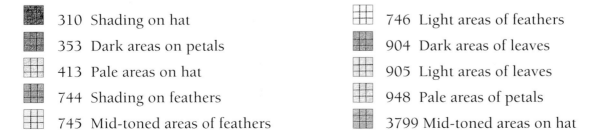

▓	310	Shading on hat	⊞ 746	Light areas of feathers
▒	353	Dark areas on petals	▦ 904	Dark areas of leaves
▦	413	Pale areas on hat	⊞ 905	Light areas of leaves
▒	744	Shading on feathers	⊞ 948	Pale areas of petals
⊞	745	Mid-toned areas of feathers	▦ 3799	Mid-toned areas on hat

Party Time

Edwardian shoes contained the most exquisite detailing with their buttons, ribbons and tapered heels. This bookmark celebrates nostalgic footwear and is a delight to stitch. Vary the colours if you prefer, but always use the same combination of dark and light shades as shown in the key.

ACTUAL DESIGN SIZE
5½ x 1¼in (14 x 3cm)

MATERIALS
- 1 piece of 18-count linen in white measuring approximately 10¼ x 6in (26 x 15cm)
- No 24 tapestry needle

INSTRUCTIONS
Mark the centre of the chart. Find the centre of your fabric and make long tacking stitches across and down. Using two strands of stranded cotton (except for backstitching where you use one strand only) begin your work following the chart. For full instructions for cross stitches, backstitches and special shaping stitches see the *Techniques* section on pages 121-126. To make the stitched piece into a bookmark, refer to the *Techniques* section on page 126.

THREADS

DMC Colour	Metres
500 dark pine green	1
501 pine green	1
502 light pine green	1
503 pale pine green	1
760 pink	1
776 pale pink	1
813 blue	1
826 royal blue	1
827 pale blue	1
838 chocolate brown	2
3328 dark raspberry pink	1
3712 strawberry pink	1
3713 pale raspberry pink	1
3820 dark yellow	1
3821 mustard	1
3822 yellow	1
3823 pale yellow	1

COLOURS FOR BACKSTITCHING
Backstitch the lace on the middle shoe using 500.
Backstitch all other outlines using 838.

Stepping out in true blue style

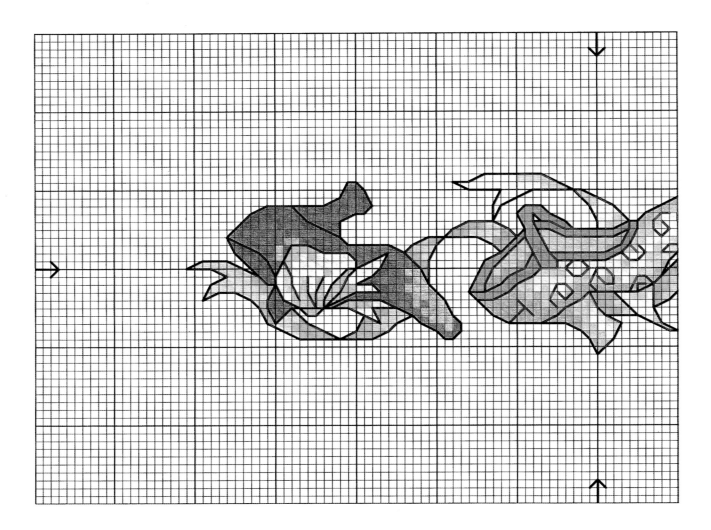

KEY

500 Strap and rim of middle shoe

501 Shading on middle shoe

502 Mid-toned areas of middle shoe

503 Pale areas of middle shoe

760 Pale areas of top shoe

776 Dark areas of ribbon on top shoe

813 Mid-toned areas of bottom shoe

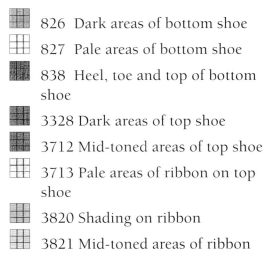

826 Dark areas of bottom shoe

827 Pale areas of bottom shoe

838 Heel, toe and top of bottom shoe

3328 Dark areas of top shoe

3712 Mid-toned areas of top shoe

3713 Pale areas of ribbon on top shoe

3820 Shading on ribbon

3821 Mid-toned areas of ribbon

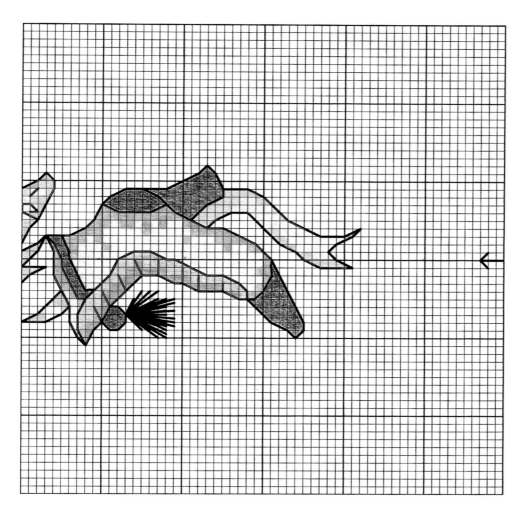

 3822 Pale areas of ribbon

3823 Palest areas of ribbon

Ribbons and Feathers

This smart burgundy hat with its feather and matching ribbon makes a delightful motif for a trinket box lid, which would look very pretty on a dressing table. The design could also be mounted in a gift card for Mother's Day if you desire. To make the ribbon decoration more exotic, stitch tiny blue beads at regular intervals along its length.

ACTUAL DESIGN SIZE
2¾ x 2¼in (7 x 5.5cm)

MATERIALS
● 1 piece of 36-count Edinburgh linen in ivory measuring approximately 7½ x 7¼in (19 x 18.5cm)
● No 24 tapestry needle
● Trinket box (optional)

INSTRUCTIONS
Mark the centre of the chart. Find the centre of your fabric and make long tacking stitches across and down. Using two strands of stranded cotton (except for backstitching where you use one strand only) begin your work following the chart. For full instructions for cross stitches, backstitches and special shaping stitches see the *Techniques* section on pages 121-126 of this book.

THREADS

DMC Colour	Metres
310 black	1
813 pale blue	1
814 burgundy	1
815 claret	1
816 maroon	1
825 deep blue	1
826 blue	1
931 slate blue	1
3753 smoky blue	1

COLOURS FOR BACKSTITCHING
Backstitch the dividing line for the bottom rim of the hat using 310.
Backstitch the hat using 814.
Backstitch the ribbon using 825.
Backstitch the feathers using 931.

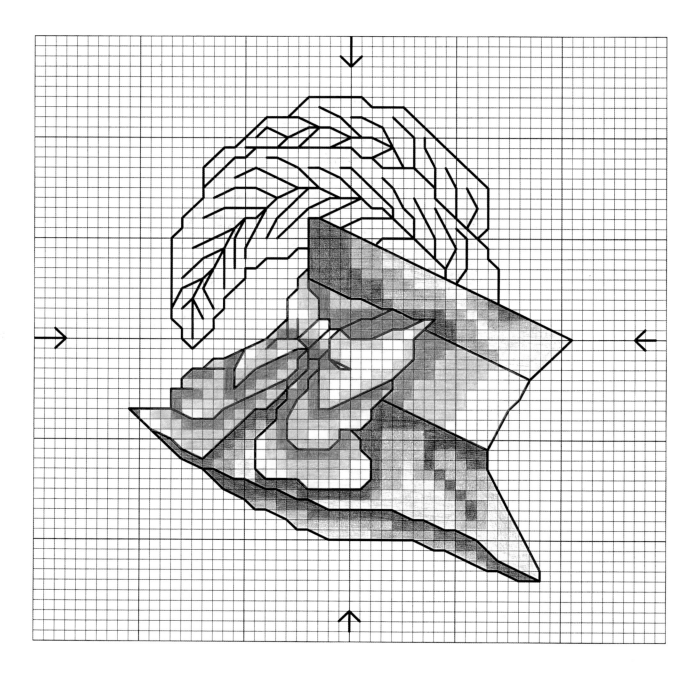

KEY

 813 Pale areas of ribbon

814 Shading on hat

815 Mid-toned areas of hat

816 Light areas of hat

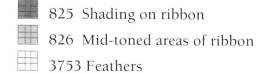 825 Shading on ribbon

826 Mid-toned areas of ribbon

3753 Feathers

A Billet-Doux

Romance never goes out of fashion, and just as a billet-doux could
send hearts fluttering with expectation, so this old-fashioned
Valentine's heart stitched in a rich deep red would make a very special
gift card for someone you love. If you like, you could embroider his and
her initials in the centre of the heart in gold backstitch.

ACTUAL DESIGN SIZE
2¾ x 2½in (7 x 6.5cm)

MATERIALS
- 1 piece of 18-count linen in white measuring approximately 7½ x 7¼in (19 x 18.5cm)
- No 24 tapestry needle
- Gift card (optional)

INSTRUCTIONS
Mark the centre of the chart. Find the centre of your fabric and make long tacking stitches across and down. Using two strands of stranded cotton (except for backstitching where you use one strand only) begin your work following the chart. For full instructions for cross stitches, backstitches and special shaping stitches see the Techniques section on pages 121-126 of this book.

THREADS

DMC Colour	Metres
304 cranberry	1
321 crimson	1
498 dark red	1
666 bright red	1
760 pink	1
761 pale pink	1
3712 strawberry pink	1
3713 pale strawberry pink	1
5284 metallic gold	1

COLOURS FOR BACKSTITCHING
Backstitch the heart using 498.
Backstitch the ribbon using 3712.
Backstitch the arrow using 5284.

The simple old-fashioned heart on this card says it all

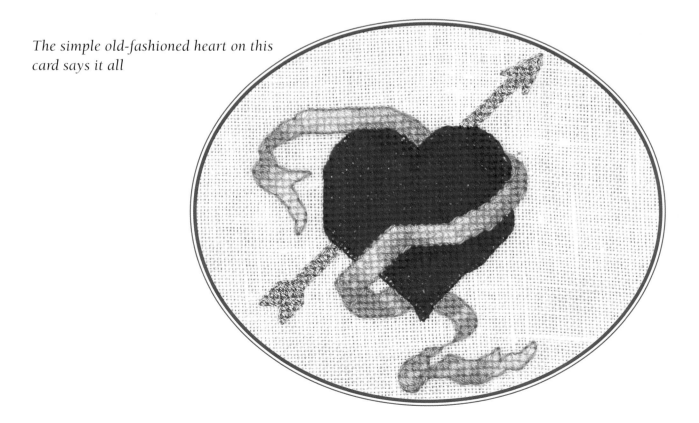

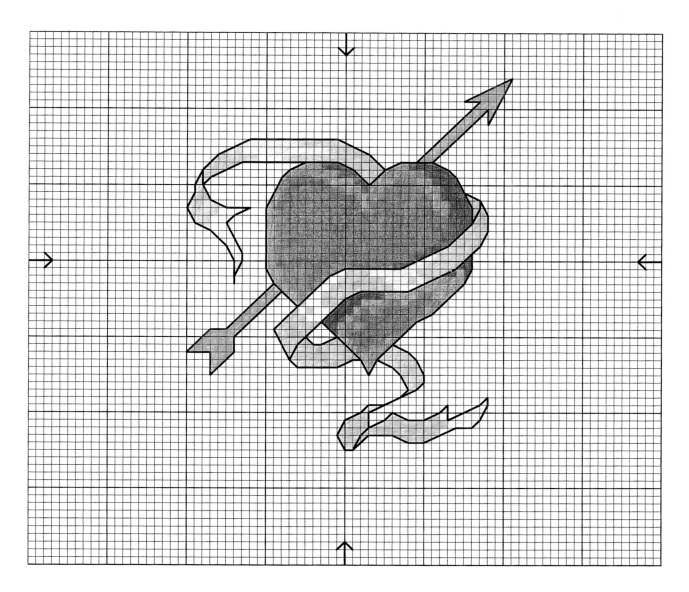

KEY

	304	Shading on heart
	321	Mid-toned area of heart
	666	Central area of heart
	760	Mid-toned area of ribbon
	761	Light area of ribbon
	3712	Shading on ribbon
	3713	Palest area of ribbon
	5284	Arrow

A Frothy Confection

This wonderful creation is a hat for special occasions. In the meantime, it is hung on a hat stand in the dressing room to keep its shape.

ACTUAL DESIGN SIZE
9¾ x 5¼in (24.5 x 13cm)

MATERIALS
- 1 piece of 18-count Aida in cream measuring approximately 14¾ x 10in (37.5 x 25cm)
- No 24 tapestry needle

INSTRUCTIONS
Mark the centre of the chart. Find the centre of your fabric and make long tacking stitches across and down. Using two strands of stranded cotton (except for backstitching where you use only one strand only) begin your work following the chart. For full instructions for cross stitches, backstitches and special shaping stitches see the *Techniques* section on pages 121-126 of this book.

THREADS

DMC Colour	Metres
350 red	2
351 dark pink	1
352 pink	2
353 light pink	3
433 dark brown	1
434 brown	1
435 dark caramel	1
469 olive green	3
470 green	3
471 light olive green	2
472 pale green	2
935 dark sage green	1
936 khaki	2
937 sage green	1
975 dark ginger	1
976 light ginger	2
977 cinnamon	1
3345 dark ivy green	1
3346 ivy green	1
3826 ginger	1

COLOURS FOR BACKSTITCHING
Backstitch the rose petals using 350.
Backstitch the feathers using 351.
Backstitch the bird using 433.
Backstitch the hat and ribbon using 937.
Backstitch the hat stand using 975.
Backstitch the leaves using 3345.

FRENCH KNOT
For bird's eye use 433.

KEY

350 Shading on petals

351 Mid-toned areas on petals, dark areas on feathers in centre

352 Dark areas on feathers at top, pale areas on feathers in centre, pale areas on petals

353 Pale areas on feathers at top

433 Wing and tail tips of bird

434 Shading on bird

435 Body of bird

469 Shading on hat

470 Dark areas of hat

471 Light areas of hat

472 Pale areas of hat

935 Shadow on underside of hat

936 Shading on rim of hat

937 Rim of hat

975 Shading on hat stand

976 Mid-toned areas of hat stand

977 Pale areas of hat stand

3345 Dark areas of leaves

3346 Light areas of leaves

3826 Dark areas of hat stand

This stitched piece would make a charming picture in a period home

Taffeta and Lace

This crinolined lady with her fan would look quite at home at an evening ball. This project is very satisfying to stitch because of the wealth of detail in the shading in the dress. For add sparkle to the picture, stitch tiny beads around the flounced hem of the dress.

ACTUAL DESIGN SIZE
7¾ x 11¼in (19.5 x 28cm)

MATERIALS
- 1 piece of 16-count Aida in white measuring approximately 12½ x 16in (31.5 x 40cm)
- No 24 tapestry needle

INSTRUCTIONS
Mark the centre of the chart. Find the centre of your fabric and make long tacking stitches across and down. Using two strands of stranded cotton (except for backstitching

The intricate shading of colours used in this design make it an extremely challenging project.

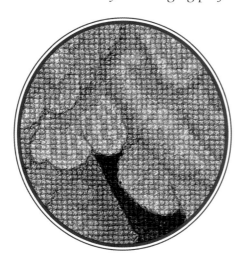

where you use one strand only) begin your work following the chart. For full instructions for cross stitches, backstitches and special shaping stitches see the *Techniques* section on pages 121-126 of this book.

THREADS

DMC Colour	Metres
433 brown	1
434 pale brown	1
435 dark caramel	1
436 caramel	4
437 fudge brown	10
738 beige	7
739 ivory	4
796 royal blue	3
797 deep blue	3
798 light royal blue	1
801 dark brown	1
820 colbalt blue	3
951 flesh pink	1
3770 pale flesh pink	1

COLOURS FOR BACKSTITCHING
Backstitch the beige area of the dress using 435.
Backstitch the fan using 437.
Backstitch the hair using 801.
Backstitch the blue area of the dress using 820.

Backstitch the face using 951.

FRENCH KNOTS
For the lady's eye use 801.

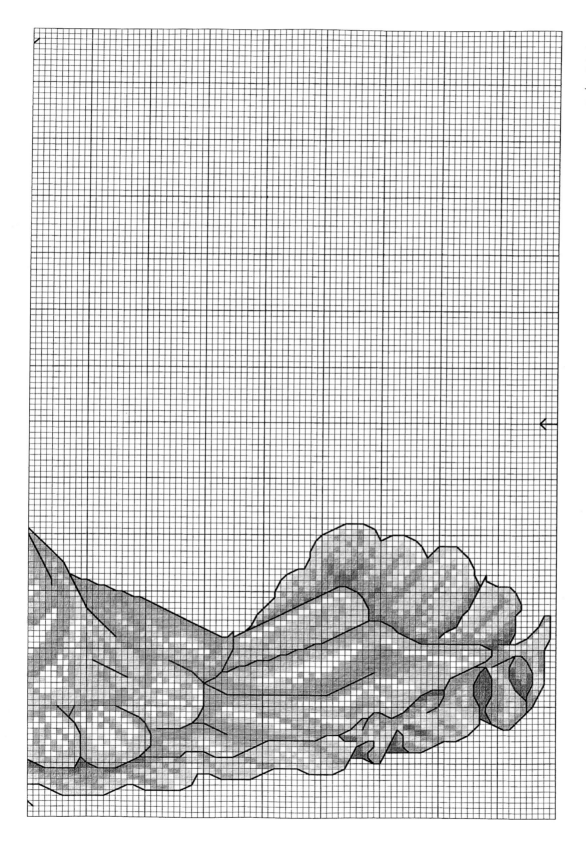

*Refer to
page 110
for the key
to this chart*

KEY

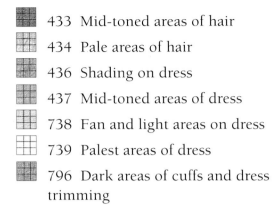

433 Mid-toned areas of hair

434 Pale areas of hair

436 Shading on dress

437 Mid-toned areas of dress

738 Fan and light areas on dress

739 Palest areas of dress

796 Dark areas of cuffs and dress trimming

797 Mid-toned areas of cuffs and dress trimming

798 Light areas of cuffs and dress trimming

801 Dark areas of hair

820 Shading on cuffs and dress trimming

951 Shading on face, neck and arm

3770 Face, neck and arm

Here you can see the delicate shading of the colours used in this challenging design

A Cameo Brooch

When dressing for dinner, a cameo brooch was the perfect ornamentation for a plain dress. If you do not possess such a brooch, this simple cameo design can be stitched in an evening then mounted in a brooch, ready for your next dinner invitation. Alternatively, you could embroider a pair of pillowslips with this motif.

ACTUAL DESIGN SIZE
1½ x 1¼in (4 x 3cm)

MATERIALS
● 1 piece of 18-count Aida in black
measuring approximately 6¼ x 6in
(16 x 15cm)
● No 24 tapestry needle

INSTRUCTIONS
Mark the centre of the chart. Find the centre
of your fabric and make long tacking stitches
across and down. Using two strands of
stranded cotton (except for backstitching
where you use one strand only) begin your
work following the chart. For full
instructions for cross stitches, backstitches
and special shaping stitches see the
Techniques section on pages 121-126 of this
book.

THREADS
DMC Colour   *Metres*
310 black   1
712 cream   1

COLOUR FOR BACKSTITCHING
Backstitch the outline of the face using 310.

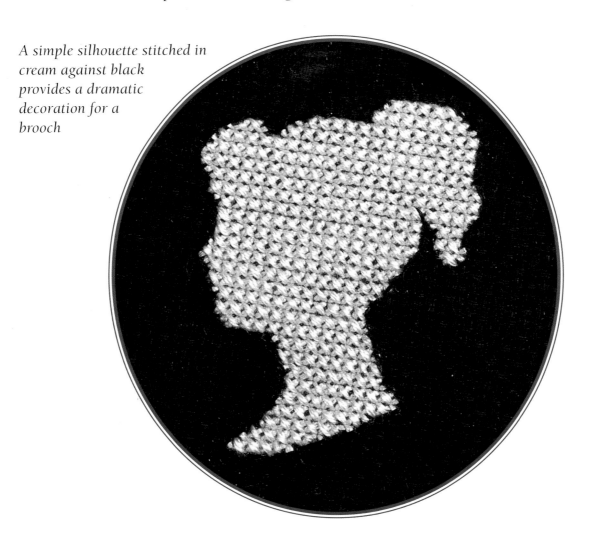

A simple silhouette stitched in cream against black provides a dramatic decoration for a brooch

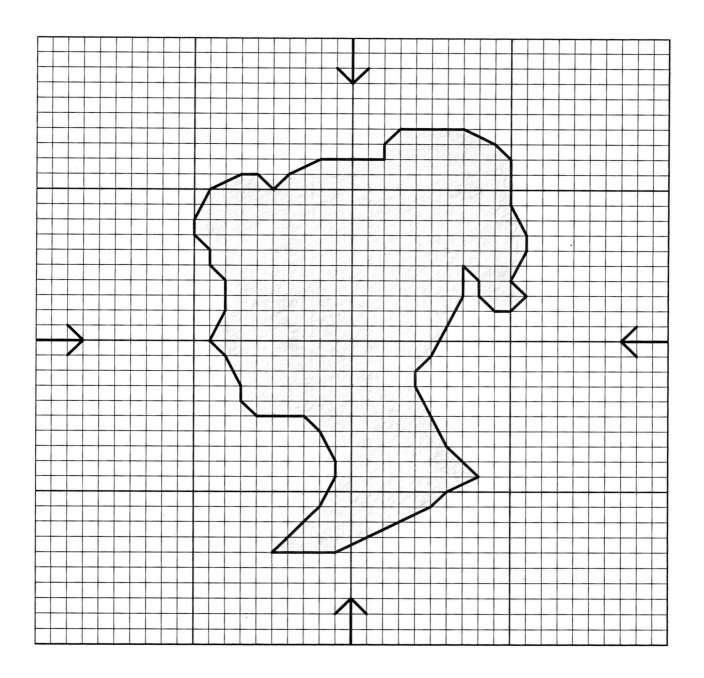

KEY

712 Entire design

Dining in Style

With their pretty drooping heads and bright colour, fuchsias are eminently suitable for decorating a Victorian-style tablecloth. The finished project is beautiful and will look pretty on any table, whatever its size, as the design is always stitched in the centre.

ACTUAL DESIGN SIZE
Octagonal ring with a diameter of 17¾in (44.5cm)

MATERIALS
- 1 piece of 11-count 'Ockav' tablecloth in white measuring approximately 32 x 32in (80 x 80cm)
- No 24 tapestry needle

INSTRUCTIONS
Mark the centre of the chart. Find the centre

This pretty fuchsia pattern will add a touch of style to any table

of your fabric and make long tacking stitches across and down. Using three strands of stranded cotton (except for backstitching where you use one strand only) begin your work following the chart. For full instructions for cross stitches, backstitches and special shaping stitches see the *Techniques* section on pages 121-126 of this book.

THREADS

DMC Colour	Metres
600 dark fuchsia	12
602 fuchsia	9
603 light fuchsia	10
604 pink	7
744 yellow	1
824 dark blue	3
825 blue	2
826 light blue	2
895 dark green	2
3345 very dark green	3
3346 green	3
3347 light green	3
3348 pale green	4

COLOURS FOR BACKSTITCHING
Backstitch the flower petals using 600.
Backstitch the stamens using 744.
Backstitch the bow using 824.
Backstitch the leaves using 895.

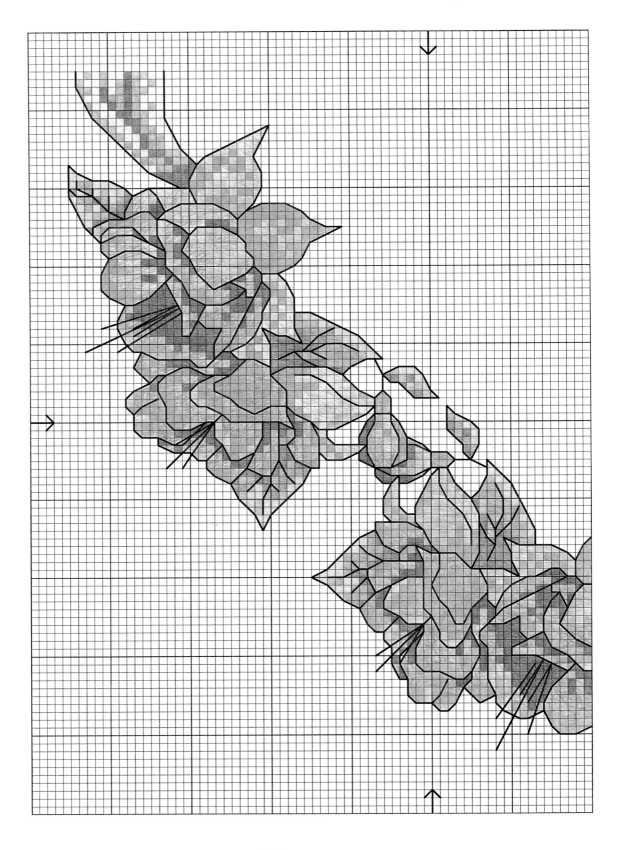

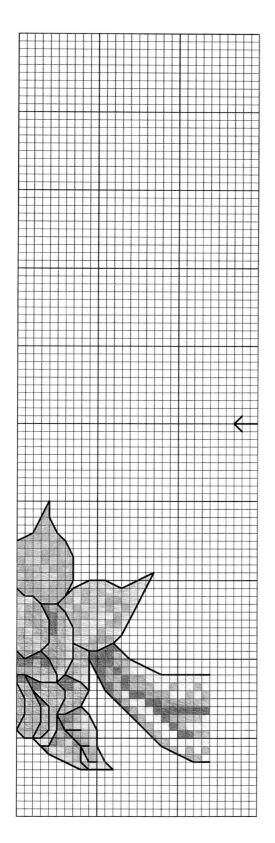

KEY

600 Shading on petals

602 Dark areas of petals

603 Mid-toned areas of petals

604 Pale areas of petals

824 Shading on ribbon

825 Mid-toned areas of ribbon

826 Pale areas of ribbon

3345 Shading on leaves

3346 Dark areas of leaves

3347 Mid-toned areas of leaves

3348 Pale areas of leaves

Refer to this pattern detail as guidance when stitching from the chart on the left

Floral Napkins

These floral napkins can be stitched to match the fuchsia tablecloth (see page 114) or to be used on their own. Alternatively, you can stitch the design for a greetings card or, using waste canvas, decorate bedlinen with the pretty fuchsia motifs.

ACTUAL DESIGN SIZE
3 x 2½in (7.5 x 6.5cm)

MATERIALS
- 1 piece of 14-count 'Oktav Napkin' Aida in white measuring approximately 16¾ x 16¾in (42 x 42cm)
- No 24 tapestry needle

INSTRUCTIONS
Mark the centre of the chart. Find the centre of your fabric and make long tacking stitches across and down. Using two strands of

Give your napkins a hint of summer with this lovely stitched fuchsia

stranded cotton (except for backstitching where you use one strand only) begin your work following the chart. For full instructions for cross stitches, backstitches and special shaping stitches see the *Techniques* section on pages 121-126 of this book.

THREADS

DMC Colour	Metres
600 dark fuchsia	8
602 fuchsia	8
603 light fuchsia	8
604 pink	8
744 yellow	1
895 dark green	4
3345 very dark green	4
3346 green	4
3347 light green	4
3348 pale green	4

COLOURS FOR BACKSTITCHING
Backstitch the petals using 600.
Backstitch the stamens using 744.
Backstitch the leaves using 895.

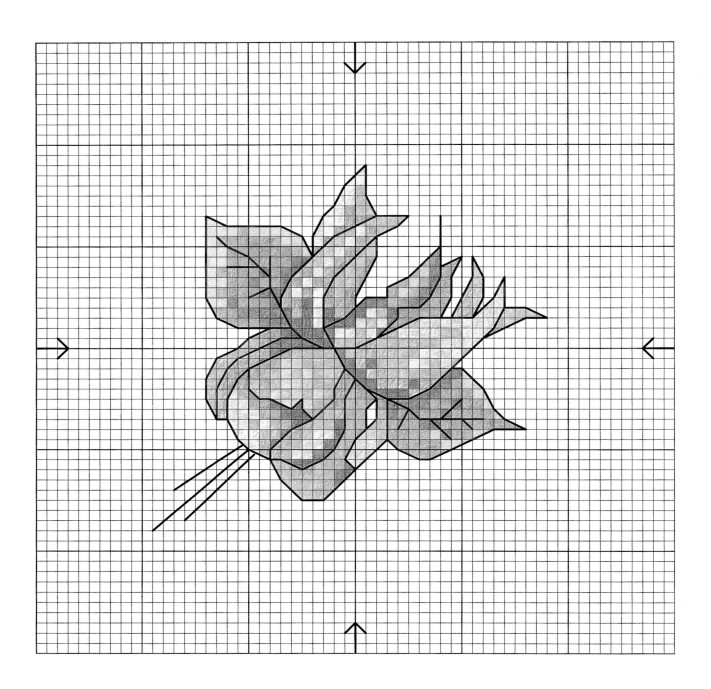

KEY

 600 Shading on petals

602 Dark areas of petals

603 Mid-toned areas of petals

604 Pale areas of petals

3345 Shading on leaves

3346 Dark areas of leaves

3347 Mid-toned areas of leaves

3348 Pale areas of leaves

Techniques

This section introduces the basic materials you need for cross stitch, and the skills you need to master – including stitching, finishing and framing – to be able to begin stitching the cross-stitch projects in this book.

TIPS

✦ Always work with clean hands.
✦ Do not drag threads across spaces where there are no cross stitches, this will show up when the piece is stretched.
✦ Let the needle hang free regularly to avoid twisting the thread.
✦ Take the work out of the embroidery hoop at night or when you stop working to avoid marking the fabric.
✦ Attach your needle to the extreme outer edge of the fabric while you are not stitching. This avoids marking the fabric.

MATERIALS

You will need to stitch on an evenweave fabric that has the same number of weft (horizontal) threads as it has warp (vertical) threads.

LINEN

This is a natural fibre so the thickness of the threads may vary across the fabric. Linen is also more expensive than Aida but as you stitch over two threads, it is much easier to use when you are stitching quarter, three-quarter and special shaping stitches. Stitching on linen produces an irregular effect.

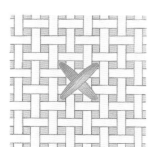

A full cross stitch worked over two threads on linen

AIDA

Beginners may find it easier to stitch on Aida fabric. The threads are woven in blocks which makes them easier to count and your stitches will look more even. You generally stitch over one block.

A full cross stitch worked over one block on Aida

WASTE CANVAS

This versatile material enables you to stitch a design onto almost anything – pillowslips, T-shirts, jumpers. Baste the waste canvas onto your chosen item and then stitch your design as normal. When you've finished, unpick the basting stitches. Gently dampen your work and pull out the waste canvas with tweezers; pull out the vertical threads first, then the horizontal threads.

DESIGN SIZE

It is important to know the 'count' of fabric you choose, as this will determine the finished size of your design. The finer the fabric, the smaller the stitches eg '18-count' Aida means there are 18 blocks to the inch, therefore producing 18 stitches to the inch. If you use '14-count' Aida your finished design will be larger as you are stitching with 14 squares to the inch. When you work on linen you stitch over two threads, so if you stitch on 32-count linen you will have 16 stitches to the inch.

Always remember to allow about 2½in (6.5cm) on each side of the design for stretching and framing.

THREADS

I have used DMC threads in my designs as the choice of colours is superb and the quality is beautiful. There are also other brands of thread available that you can use instead. However, the colours of other brands may not match the DMC colours exactly so the finished stitched piece may have a different character.

STRANDED COTTON (FLOSS)

This is made up of six strands of mercerized cotton that can be separated into single strands or groups of two or more. Most of the designs in this book are worked with two strands for cross stitches and one strand for backstitching. If you prefer a softer image, use one strand for cross stitches. Always pull one strand out at a time then put the two strands together.

PERLE COTTON

This is a mercerized thread that is non-divisible and has a soft gloss when stitched.

FLOWER THREAD

This is a non-divisible matt yarn designed mainly for work on fine fabrics, eg linen.

BE ORGANIZED

A thread organizer is invaluable. It is a piece of card with holes punched down each side. You can easily make one yourself. Once you have chosen the colours you need, cut them into 20in (50cm) or 40in (1m) lengths and thread them through the holes of the thread organizer. Label them with the colour number and when you need to use one length of thread you just remove the thread from the organizer, take off the required number of strands and replace the rest back in the thread organizer.

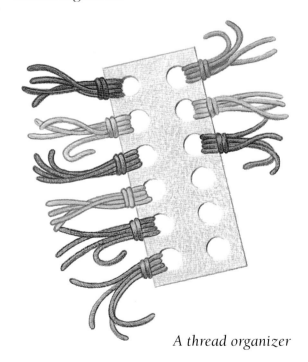

A thread organizer

FRAMES

It is personal preference whether or not you use a frame or embroidery hoop. It depends a lot on your stitching tension but as a rule, using an embroidery hoop makes stitching easier. It keeps your fabric taut and does not let it stretch and distort.

NEEDLES

For all counted needlework you will need a blunt tapestry needle. I use a size 24 tapestry needle as it is very comfortable to hold without being too thin or too chunky. For working on waste canvas you will need a crewel needle, which has a sharp point and flat eye enabling several strands to be used at once, or as required.

CHARTS

Each colour on the chart represents a colour of thread. Each square of colour represents one cross stitch. The backstitching is identified by solid lines. You will probably find it easier working in blocks of colour than rows. You will also find it helpful to have a few needles threaded with different colours, so when you change to a different colour you are ready to stitch right away.

LET'S BEGIN!

The first thing to do is find the centre of the fabric. To do this fold your fabric in half both ways. The centre is the best place to begin stitching, as your work will then be correctly positioned on the fabric. You can put long tacking stitches across and down to mark the centre to act as guidelines. Remove these when you have started your work.

All your underneath stitches must run in the same direction, so that all your top stitches will also be going the same way. Don't stitch one cross at a time unless it is a single cross stitch in a different colour to the surrounding stitches. Stitch in a row – if you have 10 cross stitches to work, stitch the 10

underneath stitches first then turn back on yourself and complete the crosses.

STARTING AND FINISHING

STARTING

Try not to use knots, as these look very unsightly when the design is finished and stretched. Anchor your thread in place by bringing your needle up through the back of the fabric where you are ready to start. Leave a tail long enough to be caught by your next few stitches and then trim the end. Look at the back of your work to check that the tail has been secured after the first few stitches.

FINISHING OFF

To finish off without using a knot, weave the thread through the backs of four or five adjacent stitches and trim the end.

CROSS STITCHES EXPLAINED

FULL CROSS STITCHES ON AIDA

To make one cross stitch, think of the stitch area as a square of four holes. Bring the needle up through the hole in the bottom left corner of the square and then down through the hole in the top right corner. Then take the needle up through the bottom right hole and down into the top left hole.

To stitch a row of cross stitches in the same colour, bring your needle up at the bottom left hole and down in the top right hole. Do not finish the stitch but continue this step until you complete the correct number of stitches going one way. Then work back along the row to complete your cross stitches, ie from bottom right to top left. Stitching in this way ensures that the line is even and regular.

FULL CROSS STITCHES ON LINEN

To stitch a single cross stitch on linen, follow the instructions as for cross stitching on Aida, but stitch across two threads of the fabric.

QUARTER STITCHES

These are indicated by a colour in a corner of a square. Work a quarter stitch as shown below. If you are using Aida, you will have to split the centre threads on the Aida with your needle. You will often find two quarter stitches in the same block but using

Quarter stitch

different colours. This is stitched very simply by stitching your first quarter stitch in one colour then, when you work your second quarter stitch in the second colour, push your needle into the same hole in the centre of the block.

If you stitch backstitches over the top after you have finished all your cross stitching, this will hide any spaces.

HALF-CROSS STITCHES

A half-cross stitch is half of a full cross stitch – in other words a diagonal stitch. It is usually used as shading in this book.

THREE-QUARTER STITCHES

I have used these stitches primarily with the special shaping stitches (described below). Work a quarter stitch as described earlier and

then make a diagonal half stitch across it to complete the three-quarter stitch.

Three-quarter stitch

SPECIAL SHAPING STITCHES

I created this stitch to give gentle sloping lines in and around the edge of the designs. It is stitched over two blocks of Aida. This is indicated on the charts by three-quarters of a square being in a colour and a quarter of the next square being in the same colour. Therefore you stitch a three-quarter stitch followed by a quarter stitch (see the illustration below). Your backstitching over the top will complete the design, shown below by a dotted line.

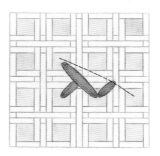

Special shaping stitch

BACKSTITCHING

Backstitching is shown on the charts by a continuous line and should be worked after the design has been completed. When the chart shows a backstitch across a cross stitch, the backstitch should be worked on the top of the stitch.

FRENCH KNOTS

These will be indicated on the chart by dots. To stitch, bring the needle up where you want the knot to be. Hold the thread as it comes out of the fabric and place the needle behind it. Twist the needle twice around the thread and insert the needle back into the fabric slightly away from where you started, keeping the thread taut all the time. Practise before stitching on your work.

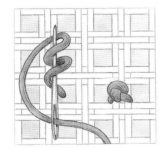

French Knot

LONG STITCHES

Long stitches are quite literally long stitches – where they are shown on the charts, just stitch that whole length with one stitch.

PETIT POINT

These stitches are stitched using one strand of floss over one thread of linen.

FINISHING

LOOKING AFTER YOUR FABRIC

It is inevitable that your work will require washing after being completed. The threads are meant to be colourfast, but to be on the safe side, take great care when washing. Immerse your work in lukewarm soapy water and gently wash by hand. Do not rub vigorously. Dry flat face down on a towel and iron on the reverse side to prevent the stitches being flattened.

LACING

Cut a piece of acid-free mount board to the same size as the inside of your frame. Centre your work on the board and insert pins along the top edge. Gently pull the fabric and pin along the bottom edge in the same way. Repeat with the sides. Turn your project over and with a large-eyed needle and crochet cotton (which must be knotted) lace the fabric from top to bottom using an under-and-over movement, ensuring that the fabric is taut. Then repeat from side to side. Stitch the corners down and remove the pins – you can now frame your work.

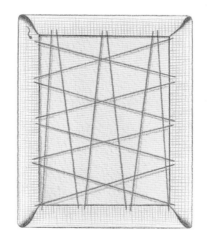

Lacing

FRAMING

MOUNTING INTO GIFT CARDS

The cards used in this book have been mounted in 3-fold cards. A wide variety are available in needlework or craft shops. Follow the individual manufacturer's instructions for mounting your work.

MOUNTING ON TO FLEXI-HOOPS

Centre your design in the flexi-hoop and place in the flexi-hoop. Trim the spare fabric on the back to 1in (2.5cm). I usually put some wadding in the middle to give some density to the picture. Lace the ends across the back of the flexi-hoop and then glue a piece of felt over them for a neat finish.

MAKING A BOOKMARK

Making sure the stitched design is central, trim the excess fabric from around the stitching so that the bookmark measures 2½ x 7in (6.5 x 17.5cm). Neaten the edges by sewing by machine or by hand. Pin a length of lace around all four edges of the bookmark, starting and finishing at the bottom edge. Mitre the lace at the corners, then stitch the lace in place. To complete the bookmark, stitch trimmings of your choice, for example, ribbons, tassels or bows, to the bottom of the bookmark, covering the join in the lace.

Acknowledgements

I would like to thank:

My husband Graham, and my three children, Danielle, David and Richard, for being patient with me even when I fall asleep over my computer in the evening and become antisocial.

Jane Prutton who worked very closely with me on this book and spent many hours and weeks designing, hand-charting initial designs and colouring in, in the way that only she can. Thank you, Jane, you have been wonderful.

Helena Mottershead for always being there with her unquestionable advice and support.

Jackie Hrycan for assisting with the charting.

Jackie Andrew for typing up all the instructions.

All my loyal stitchers who always pull out all the stops for me.

And, finally, how could I complete this Acknowledgements page without mentioning Will Napier, whose computer charting of most of the projects in this book has been fantastic. Well done, Will.

I would be totally lost without you all.

I would also like to thank the following companies for the supplies used in this book:

Framecraft Miniatures
Zweigart for their tablecloth and napkin
DMC for their threads

All the Aida and linen used in this book has been supplied by my own company, Designer Stitches UK Ltd, using 'Debbie Minton's Designer Fabrics'.

These are available from:

Designer Stitches UK Ltd
Earl Road
Cheadle Hulme
Cheshire SK8 6PQ
UK
Tel: +44 (0)161-482 6200
Fax: +44 (0)161-482 8000
Email: sales@designerstitches.co.uk

'Debbie Minton's Designer Fabrics' are available in many shades and sizes and are distributed worldwide.

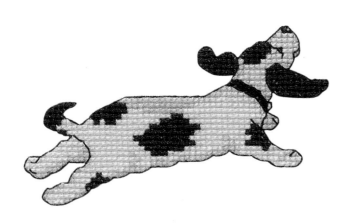